TRANSNATIONAL ENTERPRISES IN A NEW INTERNATIONAL SYSTEM

By the same author:

Direct Investment in the OECD Countries, Sijthoff & Noordhoff 1978.

TRANSNATIONAL ENTERPRISES IN A NEW INTERNATIONAL SYSTEM

Klaus W. Grewlich
Dr. jur. (Freiburg), Dr. sc. oec. (Lausanne), LL.M. (Berkeley)

SIJTHOFF & NOORDHOFF   1980
Alphen aan den Rijn, The Netherlands
Rockville, Maryland, U.S.A.

Library of Congress Catalog Card Number: 80-53754

ISBN 90 286 0650 5

Printed in The Netherlands

for Alexandre and Jérome

CONTENTS

Chapter One

INTRODUCTION

Transnational enterprises are a global issue. The emergence of these enterprises which have grown up in the last thirty years is a dramatic development of economic, social, and political significance. Transnational enterprises (TNEs) play an important part in the economies of many states and their role profoundly affects the whole spectrum of international economic relations. The future activities of these enterprises will continue to touch many concerns of international economic policy and may have particularly important economic and social implications for the two-thirds of mankind which now live in the poor countries of the world.

TNEs with global reach have developed a highly effective process of world-wide transnational decision-making which enables them to take advantage of their vast technological and marketing knowledge. As a result, these TNEs may enjoy special business opportunities in many cases.

It is widely recognized that TNEs may bring substantial benefits to host and home countries by contributing to the efficient utilization of capital, technology, and human resources; TNEs may notably play an important complementary role in the industrial development of developing countries through the transfer of resources, technology, managerial expertise, the expansion of productive capacity and employment, and the establishment of export markets. On the other hand, the use of the TNEs capacities placed at the disposal of private business policy oriented towards growth and profit may, under certain circumstances, clash with larger economic and social dimensions emerging in developed and developing countries.

It is in the interest of both governments and TNEs to avoid such clashes. One way to achieve this objective would be to set out the conditions for future relationships, i.e., to agree on a number of standards of behaviour. In drafting such standards it will be essential to recognise that the longer-term interests of the world community require that such standards induce TNEs to make an optimum contribution to development.

To be effective, such standards of behaviour must be based on a clear understanding of: (*i*) the present — real and perceived — role of TNEs in national economies and international economic relations; (*ii*) the existing governmental and intergovernmental policies designed to establish a framework tor TNE operations; (*iii*) notably, the conditions for an optimum contribution which TNEs can possibly make to world development in the context of an emerging new international economic system.

It is the purpose of this study to deal with these three areas of concern.

1. Title of study

The notion of "transnational enterprise" is used in this study to convey the idea that these enterprises operate from their home base across national borders and may also comprise state-owned enterprises.

The study prefers the expression, new international economic "system", to new international economic "order" because "system" refers much more to the idea of a long and deep process directed at reshaping the whole world system, of which the economic aspects are but a major facet.

2. Political prominences

As dramatic as the socio-economic rise of the TNEs has been their increased political prominence. The very term "transnational enterprise" implies a political visibility not associated with the words "direct investment".[1] Today the TNEs are the most visible symbol of the developed market economies and, at the same time, TNEs have become symbolic of the differences between industrial and developing countries — between the "North" and the "South".

Why are TNEs perceived in certain quarters as a potential threat? Apart from ideological explanations and from the experience that TNEs sometimes serve as a convenient whipping boy for some of the political and economic problems that trouble the world today, one answer to this question may be found in the sheer size of some of these enterprises.[2] Certain TNEs are undoubtedly a large force to be reckoned with. The $ 3 billion of value added annually by each of the top ten TNEs is greater than the gross national product of a considerable number of member states of the United Nations; and according to a well-known proposition — which has been repeated many times — 300 giant corporations will by the end of the century account for a large majority of world industrial production.[3] But even if, as other observers intimate, the future role of the TNEs is much less dramatic, the importance of TNEs as economic actors within and between nations may still imply a considerable impact — though one of varying importance — on the national economies and the international economic system. This impact may either result from direct and deliberate decisions or it may merely be a side effect of normal business activities.

TNEs carry on their business in a tightening web of regulations and controls. The capacity of even the smaller and least developed nations to impose controls on TNEs or to nationalize the local subsidiary of a TNE is an impressive indication that sovereignty is not at bay. Thus the common question of whether TNEs are likely to render the sovereignty of the nation state obsolete may to a large extent be the result of an oversimplification of the issues pertaining to the activities of TNEs. The nation state indeed continues to be the most effective regulator of TNE activities. In addition, political entities at the international level seek, within the limits of their capacities, to impose new restraints on the TNEs.

It would be an error, however, to argue that now the TNE is at bay. The actual and potential contribution of TNEs to the wealth of nations is widely recognized. Thus the prevailing objective of national policies in most countries, developed and developing, is not to keep the TNEs out, but to motivate them to make an optimum contribution to the national economy. National policies toward TNEs thus embrace two distinct dimensions: (*i*) governments seek to assert national control over the activities of resident foreign enterprises and to minimize the loss of national autonomy; and (*ii*) they also seek to increase the economic and social benefits which the TNEs may provide. Sometimes it may be difficult to reconcile these two dimensions because requirements of economic development, in which TNEs can play a very positive role, appear to conflict with the requirements of national independence.

3. Interdependence

TNEs have acquired additional dimensions in consequence of the growing prominence and interdependence of international economic relations. Due to the rapidly accelerating international economic interpenetration, economic relations among nations have moved onto a qualitatively new plane of economic and political importance.

The magnitudes of the interpenetration and interdependence of national economies have become enormous: international direct investment in terms of assets was estimated at about $500 billion for 1979; the external debt of the non-OPEC developing countries had reached $350 billion by the end of that year, the external debt of Eastern Europe (including the U.S.S.R.) was estimated, in that same year, at $45 billion; the external current account deficit of OECD countries amounted to $25 billion for 1979, whereas the OPEC countries' total surplus was estimated, by the end of 1979, at $45 billion.

The present world economic and energy problems underline the high degree of interdependence of national economies. This interdependence is, to a large extent, the result of developments which took place between 1950 and 1970: in that period of growth in industrial countries, based to a considerable extent on cheap energy, "world exports" increased over fivefold in value and now exceed $300 billion; trade has grown at an average annual rate of 10 per cent — much faster than world income. The flow of international services has increased even faster, and still more impressive have been the international capital movements, ranging from direct investment to portfolio movements and the shifts of liquid balances (despite certain control mechanisms designed to check them). But the salient feature is that the production process has become nearly as mobile among nations as trade in the goods which are exported. This applies not only to the classical "direct investment" operations but also to a wide variety of contracting arrangements.

Increasing interaction in the field of economic relations implies, however, a built-in propensity for conflict: as international economic interpenetration becomes more important and the number and complexity of domestic policy targets in the economic and social fields rise as well, international tensions are bound to increase — and this as a direct consequence of the high degree of economic interdependence. Interdependence, in fact, increases opportunities for conflict as well as cooperation, for damage as well as benefit. In short, mutual dependencies often mean mutual vulnerabilities, and governments are increasingly sensitive to this fact.

The clear understanding of the existing web of multilateral economic interaction should, of course, restrain national governments from adopting domestic economic policies which may have damaging consequences for the economic and social policies of other countries. But it is not at all certain whether understanding of interdependence and interaction will suffice to avert the danger that countries will resort to measures by which they will try to solve their own economic problems at the expense of other countries.

The world-wide operations of TNEs are an important aspect of international economic interdependence. The transnational strategies of the TNEs may, to some extent, help to integrate the world economy and to rationalize the production and distribution of the world's resources; but TNE operations may also increase mutual vulnerabilities of the nation-states. Current ef-

forts by governments to assert control over the activities of
TNEs within their territories represent one way in which governments seek to protect themselves; this relates to the question
of "economic security".

4. Economic security

While the major international security issues and challenges of
the time after the Second World War are still with us — the military race in strategic nuclear arms, the confrontation of massively
armed alliances in Europe, great power involvement in local
conflicts and in sensitive areas of the world, and the underlying
struggle of differing political systems — these are now to some
extent being overshadowed by major challenges of an economic
and socio-political nature.[4]

National security policies in today's world are designed not
merely to perform the classical tasks of foreign and defence policy, i.e., to ensure the physical survival of the individuals living
within national boundaries and to guarantee the integrity of
national territory, but also to assure some minimal expected
level of economic welfare and a certain political and social
autonomy for the nation. A major reason for this adjustment in
priorities is the deep and accelerating interpenetration and interdependence of domestic economies which has coincided, in
particular in the developed countries, with a steady proliferation of the economic and social policy objectives sought by
governments.

The basic explanation for the latter phenomenon is that societies now demand more equitable distribution of income and
increases in a vast array of social services. Thus, equality, participation, and self-management are sought in all the dimensions
of human activities in the industrialized societies — but people
look simultaneously for economic security, and government is
seen as a means of promoting the "good life".

Developing societies are particularly sensitive to issues pertaining to economic security. Although nearly all of the Third
World countries had achieved political independence by the late

1960s, a sense of powerlessness in the economic sphere remains predominant. For most of the developing countries the perception of the existing international economic system is that it is geared primarily to the interests of the developed countries. It is associated with the old political regime whereby their destiny was largely determined by outside powers.

For many states — developed and developing — the sense of threat has, to a considerable extent, shifted from the military area and the protection of the territorial integrity to the economic area.

Threats are sometimes unconventional and unintentional. It now becomes apparent why TNEs have become important in world politics, whether they wish it or not. TNEs are perceived by many developing countries — and in certain instances also by developed countries — as highly visible symbols of power and socio-economic control from outside, even though their economic power can be countered by domestic political power.

By their natures, these enterpises are supposed to exercise various degrees of control over their foreign affiliates, and their operations may have effects on jobs, price levels, growth, balance of payments policies, and, to varying degrees, on national sovereignty and security, the capacity of governments and nation states to achieve the goals of their constituents and the national self-perception in the countries concerned.

The issues pertaining to TNEs and foreign direct investment indeed cut across the whole spectrum of international economic policy: trade flows and trade policy, the monetary system, the problems and challenges relating to economic development of the developing countries, energy supply and demand, and, finally, also fundamental ideological issues such as the viability of economic liberalism and the future role of private enterprise.

By the size and spread of their commercial activities TNEs may bind nations more closely together, while simultaneously complicating their political relationships.

As to the real impact of TNEs on national economic security, there exists no general agreement as to whether the TNE is a modern form of "extra-territoriality" or whether this is just a stage in a process towards geocentric management; both alternatives would give rise to governmental concern. And there is notably no common understanding as to whether the TNE is basically exploitative or whether it is in the last resort a "benign agency" for the redistribution of wealth and the diffusion of technology and a powerful instrument in the fight for economic development.

The truth certainly lies somewhere between the extremes and each case has to be evaluated on its own merits. But even if this objective balance may be established in individual cases, it should be clearly understood that the proper perception of TNEs is in the last instance not a matter of socio-economic research and knowledge. It is a political question, and to this extent solutions must be found in the area of politics.

This explains why there do not yet exist any effective world-wide standards for international investment and for the activities of TNEs, and why there is no generally accepted machinery for the solution of political and economic conflicts to which the activities of TNEs or governmental interference in the field of direct investment may give rise.

Some TNEs may feel at ease in this muddled situation; but many TNEs recognize that it implies considerable disadvantages. In fact, the security of business transactions is at stake, because TNEs are subject to an increasing number of often conflicting laws of both the nation in which they have their "home base" and the nation in which their subsidiary does business.

Hence, there is a potential for conflict. The use of the TNEs distinctive capacities may, under certain circumstances, clash with larger political and social dimensions and the resulting potential for conflicts with national policy objectives may affect the sense of national economic security.

5. International cooperation

This is not to say, however, that all conflicts between the activities of TNEs and the policies of national governments should be interpreted as clashes between "narrow" profit-oriented business interests and larger socio-political dimensions. National governments lack, to some extent, the willingness to cooperate with other governments and to remove certain obstacles and impeding structures and, thus, the TNEs find themselves harassed by partly unnecessary impediments and restrictions that may seriously reduce their economic potential and hinder them from making an optimum contribution to the welfare of nations.

National governments may also have to make some efforts not only to look critically at, but also to a reasonable extent to learn from the TNEs which have, from the organisational point of view, indeed been remarkably successful in avoiding the sort of international frictions which have to a large degree paralyzed attempts to find an efficient solution to an increasing number of major problems in the field of international relations. There are, of course, limits to such a comparison between international business operations and the efforts of governments to organize international economic and political relations. There is, on the other hand, no doubt that there exists a need to adapt the existing political structure to the potential of modern economic reality and to prepare new forms of international cooperation, notably between the industrialized and the developing countries.

6. A new international economic system

In recent years, particularly since 1974, there has been a great deal of discussion over the conditions for a new international economic system. Some still reject the terminology "new international economic order" (used in the framework of the United Nations) as a revolutionary slogan; they prefer to speak of the reorganisation of international economic relations. Putting terminology aside, there is, however, general agreement that the main principles governing international economic relations must be re-examined, taking into account the new socio-economic situation and the changes in political attitudes and power relations over the past thirty years. International economic relations have indeed reached a crossroads: the monetary and trading systems which governed international economic relations during the first post-war generation have become fragile and can hardly be expected to govern a future world economy so different from the one for which they were constructed.

The international monetary system is no longer based on fixed exchange rates and gold; the international trading system, on the other hand, is in practice no longer based on steady reductions in barrieres to trade and non-discrimination. The number of problems which have to be tackled at the world level or at least within the framework of regional or multiregional groups will increase — hence the importance of multilateral institutions and of a new international economic system.

The economic problems of the developed countries as a whole, as well as the frictions among them[5] could probably have been important enough forces of change to lead to a new pattern in international relationships. But it was not the liberal industrialized Western world who took the initiative to shift the international mood from one of petty bargaining to one of an earnest search for synergies and convergencies in order to achieve a deep and unavoidable change in world relations. The pressure for "a new international economic order" came explicitly from the less developed countries, or rather from their most radical fractions who succeeded in uniting around it an ever-growing number of countries belonging to the Third World.

Why, under these circumstances, has the Western world not asserted its leadership and taken up this vital challenge of a global nature forcefully and credibly? It was, after all, the West which originally opened the path and led other people to follow it. It was the West which designed and dominated the present international economic system. It would, therefore, have been primarily the West's responsibility to be actively responsive to these planetary challenges for change and to start the very process of rethinking and reshaping the bases of the international political, economic and social system.

No doubt, the necessary adaptation will only be the result of a deep and long process[6] but this process cannot be allowed to be too lengthy either, nor can its beginning be delayed. Political leaders, therefore, must resist the temptation to use international meetings and conferences merely as tactical devices to play for time — which, in view of the importance of the task and the short time available, works against them. It seems, however, that on the political level in the pivotal countries of the West, there is now an increasing understanding of the spread and magnitude of these challenging problems.[7]

The fundamental question is whether the world is faced with a situation where continuous and actively pursued adjustment policies may solve most of the long-term problems within and between the industrialized societies as well as between the industrialized countries and the developing countries, or if the only viable way of reshaping international relations is to hammer out an ambitious political, economic and social system, of which the demand by developing countries for a new international economic order is but one major aspect.

One of the more important facets of the evolution of a new economic system through intergovernmental cooperation is the establishment of a balanced framework which would allow the TNEs to make an optimum contribution to world welfare and particularly economic development. The lack of generally agreed guidelines or rules concerning TNEs, including international investment (which has persisted for decades despite several efforts to overcome it) has become even more obvious with the changes in the international setting. Measures and counter-measures have been increasingly adopted by various actors in the world scene without a clear understanding of the rules of the game. It is time to deal with the problems, real and perceived, that have arisen with respect to the activities of TNEs.

If the world community cannot reach a consensus concerning the proper role of these enterprises in the framework of a new international economic system, it might, to some extent, lose a powerful instrument of innovation and an invaluable asset in the fight for economic development.

The effects and the potential of international investment and of the activities of TNEs on the longer-term structure of world politics and international economic relations thus amply justify the attention of the United Nations, which is charged by its Charter to achieve cooperation and harmonisation of nations.

But what is the quality of the relationship between TNEs and nation states? The answer to this question is one of the starting points for the idea of international cooperation in the relevant fields. TNEs and nation states are, to a certain extent, complementary institutions: one, the TNE, pursues a relatively specific set of economic objectives on a "transterritorial" basis; the other, the sovereign but territorially limited community of the nation states, seeks a broad range of political, social and economic goals. Each institution can profit from the activities of the other. But on the other hand, it is also characteristic for this relationship that a certain amount of conflict is unavoidable: The most honest corporate manager allocating resources rationally within a transnational perspective is bound to have, or there is at least a high probability that he will have, certain conflicts of interest with the most reasonable of statesmen whose rationality (and responsibility) is bounded by national interests and frontiers.[8]

But it may be equally sensible to expect that the conflicts will frequently be of a nature as to have solutions from which both parties can benefit; a basic aspect of a new international economic system will be to enhance situations in which joint gains are perceived and shared by states and TNEs. While this may be valid in many circumstances, it may be wishful thinking in others.

It should therefore be clearly stated that national communities must be allowed to decide for themselves what degree of interdependence with TNEs they find optimal and what they are willing to give for it: if, in some cases, the economic, social, and political costs of TNEs are too great, then the host countries should, of course, be free to reject the TNEs. This principle is especially important for the area which receives particularly great attention in the discussions and deliberations on a "new international economic order", i.e., the relationship of TNEs to the developing countries.

While nearly three-quarters of the activities of TNEs are concentrated in the developed market economies[9] and only the major part of the remaining quarter concerns developing countries, the focus of the on-going international discussions on the particular relationship between TNEs and developing countries is nonetheless politically justified; TNEs do indeed pose greater political problems for less developed countries, because of the difference in scale,[10] the particular sensitivity of post-colonial states, and the fact that poor countries have generally found themselves as hosts, but rarely as homes of TNEs.

The potential and real tensions and conflicts between host countries and TNEs are an important part of the background to the call for a new international economic system. The basic issues pertaining to the search for a new international economic system are directly relevant to TNEs and, by their nature, these enterprises will have to play a pivotal role within such a new economic system.

There exist some important first steps towards the elaboration of appropriate international action and arrangements with respect to the activities of TNEs and international direct investment. The current negotiations for a code of conduct under the auspices of the Economic and Social Council of the United Nations (ECOSOC) deserve particular attention.[11] Parallel work on identical or related subjects undertaken elsewhere, both within the United Nations and outside (for example, the formulation of a "code of conduct on transfer of technology" and on multilaterally agreed principles and rules for the control of restrictive business practices in the United Nations Conference on Trade and Development (UNCTAD), the "Tripartite Declaration of Principles concerning multinational enterprises and social policy" issued by the International Labour Organisation (ILO) and the "Guidelines for Multinational Enterprises" put forward by the Organisation for Economic Cooperation and Development (OECD)) underline the importance of the formulation of such rules of the game with a global or multiregional reach.

These multilateral efforts directed towards the establishment of standards or codes of conducts dealing with the issues, real and perceived, pertaining to the activities of TNEs and international investment are sometimes characterized by cynical observers as mere "public relation activities" designed to alleviate the feelings which went too high in certain quarters.

This view is certainly too narrow. It underestimates the present development. Some clarification is necessary. Why are we so modest? Why only guidelines and standards? Why should it not be possible to hammer out, within the next years — once for all — a full-fledged ambitious legal convention with broad coverage, a kind of "GATT for international direct investment"?[12]

The problem is not only one of organising very specific collective action among large numbers of states; it also stems from a basic political reality, pointed out by several authors and notably by Raymond Vernon:[13] when the basic bargain is political and may be obsolescing over time, countries consider it unwise to institutionalise a set of norms or adjudication procedures that represent only a transitory stage[14] (i.e., of the process leading to a new international economic system). Thus, the idea of continuous discussions and negotiations leading to (and later on based on) a set of non-binding guidelines, codes or "working documents" might be a realistic approach in the actual stage of development.

A very specific and once-for-all agreed-upon convention on international direct investment and the activities of TNEs would indeed presuppose that the political bargaining process between North and South has reached a consensus on the essentials of a new international economic system and that a sufficiently solid understanding of the very complex role of TNEs and international direct investment has been established. It is at least doubtful that we have reached this stage.

7. State of knowledge

It is true that research on international investment and the role of TNEs in international economic relations has increased substantially in recent years and has spread over many countries. Yet, this is taking place in an uneven manner which leaves serious gaps. As with most new disciplines, the existing stock of knowledge is not only expanding rapidly but may also be overtaken by events. The vast amount of literature with its multidisciplinary character and wide-spread fragmentation in countless scholarly and popular expositions, published and unpublished, may surpass the resources of researchers.[15] Moreover, the weeding-out process has not as yet truly begun.[16] The really new and significant is not generally separated from mere repetition and synthesis of existing knowledge; there is still a lack of basic research and frontier thinking. There exist, of course, excellent pieces of research; on the other hand, some reputable, well-documented and sophisticated contributions are not necessarily beyond challenge.

Probably it is fair to say that research on international investment today is to a large extent part of the wider discipline of "international business" and embraces international economics, the theory of the business enterprise and, to some extent, the study of government-business relations. Most of the writings on international investment and the activities of TNEs have indeed been the work of business economists and business administrators applying a management-scientific approach. In general, these have been more concerned with functional questions of finance, ownership, organisation, performance management, marketing, and less with the economics of overseas activities and the broader environmental issues. It is, however, the macro-economic and political implications of international direct investment which currently attract the attention of economists and policy makers.[17] This is sometimes classified as the "environmental approach", which is concerned with the costs and benefits of the activities of TNEs on national economies and the international economic system. Work on TNEs has thus been given new impetus in various international organisations and in particular in the United Nations, which has set up the Center on Transnational Corporations; moreover, in academic circles the problems relating to the TNEs were discovered some time ago to be a fertile field for investigation, and the traditional body of economic theory, which makes no real room for TNEs, is to some extent being re-examined.

There is a dearth of research relevant to the real problems at hand. In spite of the intensive debate over TNEs, research has, for instance, not focussed adequately on the analysis of the actual impact of the operations of TNEs on developing economies. There is a lack of problem-oriented research and of case studies[18]

which would help define the economic and social impact of
TNEs in developing countries. Streeten might, to some extent,
still be right in asserting that it is impossible to make soundly
based statements about the direction in which investments by
transnational corporations work: "A major difficulty in assessing these contributions is that far from being able to quantify
precisely these effects, we do not even know, in general, their
direction."[19] Attempts have been made to explain direct investment in terms of capital, organisation, growth, market, foreign trade, innovation, and monetary theories. These must all
compete with an increasing number of theorems with a political-
economic slant which regard investment by TNEs as related to
unequal development.

Often these studies do not differentiate between developing
countries according to their standing in the world economy and
within the Third World; such differences arise chiefly from the
relative integration in the world market and the bargaining
power of the individual developing country.

Differences between the investing TNEs in regard to capital
ownership and relative utilisation of their potential by their
headquarters must also be taken into account and attention
must be paid to the varying forms and structures with regard to
the international division of labour inside TNEs: e.g., it may be
that subsidiaries surround the parent company like satellites in a
production hierarchy, or they may participate in an intra-
groupal division of labour featuring productive specialization.[20]
Or, it may be possible for TNEs to cause capital to flow into the
host country but likewise to bring about capital outflows, to
reduce local saving and to raise the cost of capital in the host
country. They may either improve or impair the foreign exchange position of a country, depending on the volume and
structure of the reinvestments in the host country and the different forms in which incomes and profits may be transferred to
home countries. They may be able to lower or to increase the
state revenue, especially through the use they make of fiscal and
tariff policies. TNEs may adapt technologies to local conditions
or transfer technologies that may involve varying amounts of
costs for the host country. They may exercise a positive or nega-

tive influence on the terms of trade of the host country, etc., etc. In theory, there is a whole list of possible effects of the investment activities undertaken by TNEs,[21] but there is a lack of empirical evidence and, in addition, the result of the respective analysis always depends on the development model employed.

There is now comparatively more — but still not sufficient — research available on the activities of TNEs in the service sector,[22] but other issues, such as the effects of TNEs on consumer protection,[23] income distribution, certain aspects of labour relations and working standards still await in-depth analysis. These issues have to be examined in an integrated manner covering economic, social, political, and legal aspects.

There exists an obvious dilemma: on the one hand, there is no empirical basis for an intergovernmental consensus on a detailed and specific framework which would allow TNEs to make an optimum contribution to world welfare and, in particular, to economic development. It has already been explained that this is one of the reasons why it is too early to organise collective action among states towards the establishment of a specific and legally binding convention with broad coverage. On the other hand, it is impracticable to exclude a major component of the system of international economic relations from the process leading towards a new international economic system. Thus, the discussion and negotiation of a code of conduct and/or of other intergovernmental arrangements pertaining to direct investment are an important challenge which does not allow further delay. Though there is no agreement on the details, a general political consensus concerning the importance of the exercise is, of course, essential for such an undertaking which should in the final analysis certainly be more than a public relations exercise, as it should constitute a major step towards a constructive performance of TNEs in a new international economic system.

8. Design of the study

While the study makes use of existing economic knowledge it deals primarily with present and prospective policies pertaining to direct investment and TNE activities in a changing international economic system. The empirical information on which the study is based has been obtained from four sources: (*i*) qualitative and quantitative information published by governments, business organisations, trade unions and international agencies, including, in particular, the U.N. Centre on Transnational Corporations and the OECD; (*ii*) evidence provided in earlier studies; (*iii*) views and data obtained directly from the head offices of a number of TNEs and from trade unions; considerable effort was expended in collecting information from business firms that invested in developing countries; (*iv*) a series of personal discussions with business and trade union representatives and government officials, in particular from developing countries.

The emphasis of the study is on the development of standards for direct investment and TNE activities in a new international economic system. While the study is based on detailed knowledge of existing codes of conduct and other instruments in the field of international investment and notably on experience with the negotiations underway in the U.N. framework, its purpose is not to anticipate the precise outcome of these negotiations by proposing a full -fledge "Code of Conduct". The objective of the study is to deal with the basic philosophical choices which have to be made in order to establish a balanced set of standards for international investment and TNE activities. The substantive proposals are thus designed to exemplify the basic philosophy.

The study is future-oriented and prospective. It deals, to some extent, with the evaluation of the present impact of TNE activities in developed and developing countries and with the approaches taken by concerned parties, notably the governments. But its main purpose is to explore the general framework of the future economic system and the role of international investment, including its modern forms like franchising and contracting in the new economic system.

The basic point of reference for the study is the plight of some 800 million individuals trapped in a miserable life characterised by malnutrition, disease and hideous surroundings. This is the touchstone in making the decisions for the new economic system and outlining the roles which the different components of the system have to play in the future.

The study is based on both the economic theory and the empirical fact that economic liberalism and entrepreneurial freedom in international economic relations, subject to adequate social corrections and limitations reflecting the particular needs of developing countries, may allow TNEs to make an effective contribution to world development. It is the purpose of the standards to establish the right balance between freedom and responsibility, between liberalism and protection of the weaker party, between the uncontrolled exercise of sovereign rights and protection of entrepreneurial confidence.

There is a chance that the U.N. Code of Conduct, which is under discussion in the Commission on Transnational Corporations, will be ready in the near future. This would, however, not make the considerations and findings of this study obsolete, in particular, because:

—the substantive scope of the proposed standards is wider than the prospective U.N. Code of Conduct;

—it is very likely that the U.N. Code will be only a first step in a continuous process of multilateral discussions and negotiations in the framework of a much broader and deeper development towards a new international economic system, the prospective basic philosophical orientations of which are set out in the present work.

The study considers in Part One definitional and methodological questions and issues relating to trends, determinants and impacts of TNE activities.

The main developments and issues pertaining to national policies and international approaches in the field of direct investment and TNE activities are discussed in Part Two; this part presents, notably, a categorisation of international responses to TNE operations.

Part Three deals with the process directed towards a prospective new international economic system[24] and elaborates, on this basis, on a world-wide framework for direct investment and TNEs, designed to allow TNEs to make an effective contribution to world development.

The views expressed and that facts stated in this study are the sole responsibility of the author.

Notes to chapter one

1. Cf. Vernon, *Sovereignty at Bay*, 1971; Nye, "Multinational Corporations in World Politics," *Foreign Affairs*, vol. 53 (1974), p. 153; Dunning, *Studies in International Investment*, 1970, p. 12.

2. Cf. The statistical material in U.N. ECOSOC Commission on Transnational Corporations, *Transnational Corporations in World Development: A Re-examination*, E/C.10/38 (1978).

3. Nye, op. cit., p. 153.

4. Mondale, "Beyond Détente: Toward International Economic Security," *Foreign Affairs*, vol. 53 (1974), p. 1.

5. See Bergsten, *The Future of the International Economic Order: An Agenda for Research* (1), 1973)

6. This process would not only concern the issue of a new international economic system, but also other vital problems such as the natural environment, basic resources, the state of society and the violence complex; cf. Peccei, "An interpretation of world situations and prospects," *Forum for Correspondence*, vol. 9 (1978), p. V-91; Tinbergen, "The Need for an Ambitious Innovation of the World Order," *Journal of International Affairs*, vol. 31 (1977), p. 305.

7. Cf. for instance "OECD Ministers agree on concerted action for growth and intensified development cooperation" (OECD Ministerial Council 1978), *OECD Observer*, no. 93 (1978) p. 4; also "Communiqué issued July 17th, 1978 in Bonn at the end of a summit conference attended by the heads of government of seven industrial nations and the president of the European Community Commission," *Wireless Bulletin from Washington*, no. 135 (1978) p. 1. The results of UNCTAD V on the other hand are not too encouraging.

8. Nye, op. cit., p. 168.

9. U.N. ECOSOC Commission on Transnational Corporations, *Transnational Corporations in World Development: A Re-examination*, E/C. 10/38 (1978), p. 8.

10. General Motors' annual profits exceed the annual income of most African states.

11. These negotiations take place in the framework of the Commission on Transnational Enterprises which was set up by ECOSOC Resolution 1913 (LVII) of 5 December 1974.

12. Kindleberger and Goldberg, "Towards a GATT for Investment: A Proposal for Supervision of the International Corporation," *Law and Policy in International Business*, 2 (Summer 1970).

13. Vernon, *Sovereignty at Bay*, 1971, p. 46.

14. This might be one of the reasons why a number of countries have refused to join the International Center for the Settlement of Investment Disputes which has been established by the World Bank.

15. See U.N. ECOSOC Commission on Transnational Corporations, *Research on Transnational Corporations*, U.N. Doc. E/C. 10/12 (1976) and Annex U.N. Doc. E/C. 10/12/Add. 1 (1976); *Survey of Research on Transnational Corporations* (survey conducted by the Center on Transnational Corporations), ST/CTC/3 (1977).

16. U.N. ECOSOC Commission on Transnational Corporations, *Research on Transnational Corporations*, op. cit., p. 49.

17. Dunning, op. cit., p. 12; see, for instance, two studies which have been prepared for the use of policy-makers; Department of Trade and Industry (U.K.), *The impact of Foreign Investment on the United Kingdom*, 1973; and Government of Canada, *Foreign Direct Investment in Canada*, 1972.

18. E.g., Iffland and Galland, *Les investissements industriels suisses au Mexique*, 1978.

19. Streeten, "The Theory of Development Policy," John H. Dunning (ed.), *Economic Analysis and the Multinational Enterprise*, London 1974, p. 257.

20. Cf. Jungnickel, "Die Wettbewerbsposition der deutschen multinationalen Unternehmen im internationalen Vergleich — Wachstum, Effizienz und Internationalisierungsstrategie," Däubler und Wohlmuth (ed.), *Transnationale Konzerne und Weltwirtschaftsordnung*, 1977.

21. Wohlmuth, "Transnational Corporations and International Economic Order," *Intereconomics*, no. 9, 10 (1977), p. 237.

22. Cf. U.N. ECOSOC Commission on Transnational Corporations, *Transnational Corporations in World Development: A Re-examination*, op. cit., (for instance) p. 46.

23. While special attention may be given to the role and impact of TNEs in industries particularly relevant to consumers, such as food processing and the pharmaceutical industry, the studies relating to this field should not be confined to TNEs activities; see in this context, ECOSOC, *Consumer Protection: A Survey of Institutional Arrangements and Legal Measures*, E/1978/81.

24. The final version of the report of the Independent Commission on International Development Issues (Brandt Commission), *North-South: A programme for survival*, 1980, has been published after conclusion of the present study.

Part one

The activities of transnational enterprises

Chapter Two

DEFINITIONS

The issue of defining "international investment" and "transnational enterprises" is rather complex; it has found its expression in countless publications and reports.

1. "International investment"

The term "international direct investment" implies that the phenomenon is being considered from a global perspective. From the viewpoint of the individual countries affected by international investment flows, it might be preferable to use the notion of "foreign direct investment". A distinction might be drawn between inward and outward direct investment, allowing for an assessment of the impact of inward direct investment on the national economy, it being understood that any act of direct investment is both an outgoing direct investment (in the eyes of the source country) and an incoming direct investment (in the eyes of the recipient country). Another important distinction is that between the initial once-for-all effect of an inward investment and the continuing effects which arise because the investment, i.e., the enterprise, is owned and operated by foreigners. Finally, one would have to distinguish between "green-field investment" and the take-over of a national firm.

With regard to manufacturing in developing countries, three categories of private foreign investment may be distinguished: (i) export-oriented investment, intended primarily for the purpose of supplying exports from developing countries, in many cases for inclusion in a final product assembled in another country and based mainly on the availability of cheap labour or some other cheap resources in the host countries; (*ii*) market-development investment, intended mainly to produce output for sale in the host country and directed toward the future development of the market to an economic size with production costs which would be internationally competitive; and (*iii*) investment which is initiated and subsidised actively by the host country, sometimes with little or no reference to present and prospective levels of demand and comparative costs and frequently designed mainly to displace imports.[1]

In general, by direct investment is meant an investment in a foreign country where the investing party (enterprise) retains or expands control over the investment. A direct investment typically takes the form of a foreign enterprise starting a subsidiary or taking over control of an existing firm in the country in question. The OECD Code of Liberalisation of Capital Movements defines direct investment as "investment for the purpose of establishing lasting economic relations with an undertaking such as, in particular, investments which give the possibility of exercising an effective influence on the management thereof." The definition thus centres upon concept of control and leaves it to governments — which have varying criteria in this regard — to decide what level of foreign participation in the capital of an enterprise constitutes a direct rather than a portfolio investment. Control is usually determined on the basis of ownership and in this connection the *Balance of Payments Manual*[2] has suggested as a possible criterion of control the ownership , by a closely associated group, of 25 per cent or more of the voting stock (or ownership rights) of the enterprise in which the investment is made.

It should be made clear, on the other hand, that a grasp of the concept of control is not sufficient to fully understand the phenomenon of direct investment: in many cases it is indeed not so much a movement of capital involved in a direct investment as an international movement of technique or organisation. Frequently capital is only the complementary factor of production in a direct investment.[3] The transfer of technology will become even more important in the future to the extent that the "classical" direct investment operations are supplemented or replaced by different forms of contracting.

In view of the importance of the international comparability of the balance-of-payments data, including direct investment, reported by individual countries, the International Monetary Fund (IMF) has elaborated a standard reporting system providing definitions for the various transactions so that they might be uniformly classified by national reporting agencies. Although applying specifically to direct investment flows, these definitions or concepts are useful not only for the purpose of classifying the relevant international transaction but also for the compilation of direct investment stock data. The standard presentation of the IMF balance-of-payments statistics for direct investment flows includes: investment in branches; acquisition of common stocks of the direct investment enterprise; inter-company debts; and undistributed earnings. In addition to that, the IMF classification also provides for the separate reporting of foreign investment in direct investment enterprises which is not itself direct investment capital. Such investments may have some of the characteristics of regular portfolio investment, but they may also carry with them some influence on the operation of the enterprise or be undertaken because of the existence of foreign control. Some countries include such investments in their compilation of direct investment stock data.[4]

While some degree of standardisation has been achieved with respect to the reporting of direct investment flows, considerable diversity still exists with respect to the compilation by governments of direct investment stock data. The differences result from such factors as differences in definition and the coverage and scope of data. Furthermore, while the majority of countries include in their annual balance-of-payments statement some data on direct investment flows, only a limited number of countries compile and publish direct investment stock data on a regular basis. A few, though an increasing number, of the developing countries collect and publish periodically statistics on the stock of foreign direct investment in their own economies.

There may be a number of reasons to explain the differences in methodology and coverage of direct investment stock data but there is no doubt that the resultant lack of comparability of direct investment stocks[5] renders the overall appraisal of the size, growth and interrelationships of the operations of TNEs on the basis of direct investment figures rather difficult and virtually impossible in some respects.[6]

2. "Transnational enterprises"

It is necessary to make a distinction between the concept of international direct investment and that of the TNE, as international direct investment does not necessarily give rise to the questions met with in considering the activities of TNEs — although similar problems might appear in certain cases.

There is no agreed definition of what constitutes a TNE. The simplest approach in thinking about the subject may be to recognize that there is a continuous spectrum of companies, depending on how far their activities are exclusively national and how far they are international. At the one end, there is the clearly national enterprise which simply exports its products; as a natural development, this company may set up selling subsidiaries and later on production subsidiaries in foreign countries. At the other extreme, there exists what everyone would recognize as a TNE, which operates on a substantial scale in many countries producing, distributing and investing, and which plans its policies of capital investment, research, sales and distribution on a world scale, taking a global view distinct from that of any single national enterprise within its system.[7]

From a theoretical point of view it might be said that international investment is a narrower concept than the TNE. The analysis of the former is essentially concerned with the economics of operating over-the-border activities which involve the transfer of capital and with the impact on host and home countries as well as on the international economic system, but it is only incidentally concerned with organisational or administrative aspects and the wider aspects of the political prominence of certain direct investment activities. By contrast, a consideration of the activities of TNEs is multidisciplined and used to be more concerned with the factors — political, sociological and legal, as well as economic — influencing the process of decision-making and business policy, i.e., of managing and organizing the enterprise; it is now, to a large extent, concerned with the costs and benefits of the activities of TNEs on the national economies and the international economic system.

2.1. *Survey of definitions*

The number of plausible definitions of the TNE is large. The criteria used in these definitions cover a wide spectrum and the range and spread multiplies when various criteria are combined. There exist criteria with regard to the degree of transnationality (emphasizing such features as a minimum number of foreign affiliates or the spread across continents), ownership, the organisational form, sector and activity, size, etc. A comparison of various definitions containing different criteria used in various connections reveals that they are, in general, closely related to the purpose at hand. Thus, e.g., for the issue of restrictive business practices, the degree of central control to which the component units of a TNE may be subject will be of special importance; in the field of technology transfer the emphasis is naturally on the technological potential of the respective TNE; for questions relating to manpower and social affairs the number of employees is particularly significant.

Dunning has developed the following definition which is, however, restricted to producing enterprises: "The concept of the international or multinational producing enterprise (MPE) ... (is defined) simply as an enterprise which owns or controls producing facilities (i.e. factories, mines, oil refineries, distribution outlets, offices, etc.) in more than one country."[8] Well known is Perlmutter's distinction between ethnocentric (or home country-oriented), polycentric (or host country-oriented) and geocentric (or world-oriented) TNEs;[9] while the enterprises never appear in these pure forms, the distinction may be, nevertheless, helpful as a theoretical tool for analytical purposes. Professor Goetschin has developed a very helpful framework allowing for a deeper understanding of the different stages in the process of "multinationalisation."[10] Goetschin distinguishes the following stages: national, international, transnational, multinational and supranational; each stage having its particular characteristics with regard to ownership, chartering, distribution of shares, origin of sales and management. In his book *Sovereignty at Bay* Vernon presents the following comments:

> a multinational enterprise [is] ... a parent company that controls a large cluster of corporations of various nationalities. The corporations that make up each cluster appear to have access to a common pool of human and financial resources and seem responsive to elements of a common strategy. Size is important as well; a cluster of this sort with less than $100 million in sales rarely merits much attention. Moreover, the nature of the group's activities outside its home country is relevant...; finally, the enterprises involved generally have a certain amount of geographical spread; a parent with a stake in only a country or two outside its home base is not often found on the list (of multinational enterprises).[11]

Finally, there is the utopian vision of George Ball who expects the global chartering of TNEs:

> ...world corporations (which) should become quite literally citizens of the world. What this implies is the establishment by treaty of an international company law, administered by a supranational body, including representatives drawn from various countries, who should not only exercise normal domiciliary supervision but would also enforce anti-monopoly laws and administer guarantees with regard to uncompensated expropriation.[12]

From a practical point of view there exist two basic options to clarify what is actually meant by "multinational enterprise," "transnational corporation" or "TNE":[13]

—Drawing up a nominal list of enterprises doing business in a certain number of countries, based on the level of ownership or closeness of contractual links (which would, in particular, result in a "local company" being deemed to be under the effective control of its parent company) and on additional criteria such as sectors of activity, minimum size (average of activity, etc.), size of component, nature of component, qualitative criteria (nationality of management, company strategy, etc.);

—Starting from the concept of direct investment and hence including all enterprises carrying on activities in more than one country, with due regard to certain criteria such as minimum size, threshold of foreign participation, mobility, etc. If no particular criteria are applied, most acts of direct investment would regularly involve an enterprise operating business in two or more countries; such a definition of the TNE would, of course, be very closely linked with the definition of direct investment. Thus the approach followed by the Commission of the European Communities was to take into consideration all foreign direct investment "80 per cent of which is certainly due to undertakings intuitively recognized by all as multinationals."[14] One issue in this context is, however, whether major enterprises, such as Lockheed or Dassault, which export heavily but own no assets outside their home country, should be treated as TNEs because of their large volume of exports.

While a considerable number of proposals with regard to the definitional problem have been made from different sides, international organisations, such as the U.N., OECD, ILO, and the EEC, concerned with operational issues pertaining to the activities of TNEs and international direct investment, have so far neither established a precise legal definition nor developed a set of definitions to be respectively applied with regard to the varying purposes at hand.

All of these international organisations have, however, so far abandoned the idea of establishing a voluntary register for TNEs, as they came to the conclusion that TNEs in general did not really have any interest in putting their names on the register.

The idea of a nominal list, on the other hand, being limited to the "big TNEs" to which public concern is of course basically related, was dropped because of the difficulty in establishing a nonarbitrary cut-off point. In addition, it became evident in the course of the discussions at the international level that, while it was clearly the activities of TNEs which gave rise to concern — real or perceived — other enterprises are in many cases able to operate in the same manner and raise the same sort of problems. Any consideration of remedial action (for instance, by the establishment of a code of conduct) would have to take account of this important aspect in order to avoid the reproach of arbitrary and discriminatory treatment of a special group of enterprises. Thus, it might, in fact, be too early for a precise legal definition for operational purposes. On the other hand, a clarification of the term "transnational enterprises," "transnational corporations," or "multinational enterprises" is, of course, necessary for statistical purposes.

In the course of the discussions that led to the OECD Declaration and Decisions of 21 June 1976 containing the OECD Guidelines for Multinational Enterprises,[15] the OECD Committee on International Investment and Multinational Enterprises concluded as follows:

> A precise legal definition of multinational enterprises is not required for the purposes of the Guidelines. These usually comprise companies or other entities whose ownership is private, state or mixed, established in different countries and so linked that one or more of them may be able to exercise a significant influence over the activities of others and, in particular, to share knowledge and resources with the others. The degree of autonomy of each entity in relation to the others varies widely from one multinational enterprise to another, depending on the nature of the links between such entities and the fields of activity concerned. For these reasons, the guidelines are addressed to the various entities within the multinational enterprise (parent companies and/or local entities) according to the actual distribution of responsibilities among them on the understanding that they will cooperate and provide assistance to one another as necessary to facilitate observance of the guidelines. The word "enterprise" as used in these guidelines refers to these various entities in accordance with their responsibilities.

This attempt to clarify the notion of the TNE contained in the OECD Guidelines deserves greater attention, as it may be used as a reference point for the discussions and deliberations underway in other international fora such as, in particular, the U.N. ECOSOC Commission on Transnational Corporations.

In adopting this part of the Guidelines, OECD countries have followed a pragmatic approach. They have recognized that the TNE is basically a socio-economic phenomenon and not a legal institution as such and that a description of a TNE in legal terms would not be adequate for the purpose of laying down voluntary guidelines to be observed by TNEs. The formula thus used is distinguished, in fact: (*i*) by a wide coverage of companies whose ownership may be private, state or mixed ("companies or other entities"), the legal form of a company is thus not decisive; (*ii*) by the possibility that one or more of these companies may be able to exercise significant influence over the others; and, (*iii*) by the possibility of sharing knowledge and resources with the other parts of the company or entity. This formula recognises that the degree of autonomy of each entity in relation to the others varies widely according to the actual set-up of the company which itself is a function of the activities in which these enterprises engage. It is most important to realise that the Guidelines are not merely addressed to the parent company or to the TNE as a whole, but in a very pragmatic way to the various entities within the TNE according to the actual distribution of responsibilities with the understanding that these various entities will cooperate and provide assistance to one another as necessary to facilitate observance of the Guidelines. This formula is, in fact, some sort of "those-who-are-concerned" approach: the OECD Guidelines would apply to those TNEs, i.e., their respective component units, which in the concrete instance are in a position to observe them (or to violate them); this is made particularly clear by the last sentence of the definitional part of the OECD Guidelines, which says that the word "enterprise" as used in these Guidelines refers to the various entities within the TNE in accordance with their responsibilities.

While the OECD Guidelines are limited to the OECD area,[16]

the Tripartite Declaration of Principles Concerning Multinational Enterprises and Social Policy adopted by the Governing Body of the International Labour Office (ILO) on the basis of a Tripartite Consultative Meeting on Relations between Multinational Enterprises and Social Policies[17] contains a set of principles dealing with the social aspects of TNE activities, particularly in developing countries. The ILO Declaration contains, in paragraph 6 of the preamble, a description of the TNE which rather closely follows the OECD approach. Furthermore, like the OECD Guidelines, the Declaration states that:

> the principles laid down in this Declaration do not aim at introducing or maintaining inequalities of treatment between multinational and national enterprises. They reflect good practice for all. Multinational and national enterprises, wherever the principles of this Declaration are relevant to both, should be subject to the same expectations in respect of their conduct in general and their social practices in particular.

In this way the ILO Declaration attempts to get rid of the thorny problem of defining TNEs.

At the present stage of discussions in the United Nations Commission on Transnational Corporations, a specific definition of transnational corporations has not been developed as yet. However, the definition contained in the report of the group of Eminent Persons[18] is considered in some quarters, i.e. most industrialised countries, as an adequate formula; this, of course, would leave open the possibility of developing more specific and narrower definitions, as required, in the course of the formulation of the code of conduct.[19] Others believe that the definition should be based on a certain number of criteria, such as size, multiplicity of operations, central decision-making or global strategies; that the evolution of such criteria should commence right away; and that this should lead to a U.N. list of TNEs. The group of Eminent Persons, in their report entitled "The Impact of Multinational Corporations on Development and on International Relations" has used a broad definition, namely: "Multinational corporations are enterprises which own or control production or service facilities outside the country in which they are based. Such enterprises are not always incorporated or private; they can also be cooperatives or state-owned entities."[20]

2.2. *Clarifying remarks*

The description and analysis of the various attempts to define the TNE have shown the complexity of the issues. It has become clear that there exist many proposals and suggestions, but that on the operational side not much progress has been made. For the purpose of the following study, a number of clarifications are necessary:

—This study generally uses the rather wide notion of TNEs along the lines of the OECD approach and the definition used by the Eminent Persons; this does not exclude the fact that in certain cases the study will focus particularly on the "big TNEs" or a special group of TNEs.

—There exist no basic differences between the notions of "multinational" and "transnational". The word "transnational", however, better conveys the notion that the enterprises under consideration operate from their home bases across national borders.

—The study uses the word transnational "enterprises" (TNEs) and not "corporations" in order to underline the fact that TNEs may also comprise state-owned enterprises. There exist today many state-owned, profit-seeking enterprises, which in fact behave like TNEs in many respects. In addition, the term "enterprise" is preferred to "corporation" in order to convey the idea that the legal form of the undertaking, i.e. whether it is incorporated or not, is from a functional point of view of no significance.

—As there is no widely accepted definition of the "TNE", the study uses, in most instances, the notion "international investment and the activities of TNEs," which recognises the fact that most acts of direct investment normally involve an enterprise operating business in two or more countries; at the same time, this juxtaposition allows to keep in mind the socio-economic and political prominence of the subject; finally, this notion may be flexible enough to also embrace alternatives to the "classical" form of direct investment which include, in particular, specific contractual arrangements.

Notes to chapter two

1. Reuber, *Private Foreign Investment in Development*, 1973, p. 8.
2. International Monetary Fund, *Balance of Payments Manual*, 3rd ed. (Washington, D.C., 1961, reprinted 1966).
3. Cf. Södersten, *International Economics*, 1971, p. 444; Goetschin, "L'entreprise multinationale — présent et futur," *Revue économique et sociale*, 31ème année, no. 1 (1973), p. 8; Bertrand, *Economie Financière Internationale*, 1971, p. 49.
4. A general survey of the data on direct investment compiled by different developed market economies is contained in ECOSOC Commission on Transnational Corporations, *Transnational Corporations in World Development: A Re-examination*, E/C.10/38 (1978), Annex VII.
5. Except in the single case of United States and Canadian data, which are by their nature closely interrelated.
6. ECOSOC Commission on Transnational Corporations, *Transnational Corporations in World Development: A Re-examination*, op. cit., p. 342.
7. Cf. OECD, *Policy Perspectives for International Trade and Economic Relations* (Rey Report), 1972.
8. Dunning (ed.), *The Multinational Enterprise*, London 1971, p. 16.
9. See Perlmutter, "The Tortuous Evolution of the Multinational Corporation," *Columbia Journal of World Business*, vol. 4 (1969), p. 11.
10. Goetschin, "L'entreprise multinationale — présent et futur," op. cit., p. 10/11.
11. Vernon, *Sovereignty at Bay*, 1971, p. 4. Vernon has continuously refined these considerations in the framework of Harvard's Multinational Enterprise Project which studied the spread and dimensions of 187 American TNEs in the raw materials and manufacturing industries; see Vernon, *Storm over Multinationals: The Real Issues*, 1977.
12. Ball, "Cosmocorp: The Importance of being Stateless," Brown (ed.), *World Business*, 1970, p. 337.
13. The U.N. Center on Transnational Corporations currently collects all available definitions on TNEs; a certain number of definitions are contined in United Nations, *Multinational Corporations in World Development*, ST/ECA/190 (1973), p. 118.
14. EEC (Commission), *Multinational Undertakings and Community*

Regulations, Communication from the Commission to the Council presented on 8th November, 1973, *Bulletin of the European Communities — Supplement 15/73*, Brussels 1973, p. 21.

15. OECD, *International Investment and Multinational Enterprises*, 1976.

16. Members of OECD are, Australia, Austria, Belgium, Canada, Denmark, Finland, France, The Federal Republic of Germany, Greece, Iceland, Ireland, Italy, Japan, Luxembourg, The Netherlands, New Zealand, Norway, Portugal, Spain, Sweden, Switzerland, Turkey (the Turkish government did not participate in the Declaration), the United Kingdom and the United States.

17. The Tripartite Consultative Meeting (eight governments, eight employers' and workers' members) took place in Geneva on 4-7 April 1977. "The Tripartite Declaration of Principles Concerning Multinational Enterprises and Social Policy" was adopted by the Governing Body of the International Labour Office on 16 November 1977.

18. The group of Eminent Persons ... to study the role of multinational corporations and their impact on the process of development ... was established by ECOSOC Resolution 1721 (LIII) adopted on 2 July 1972.

19. See *The CTC* (Center on Transnational Corporations) *Reporter*, vol 1, no. 2 (1977), p. 10; cf. also Commission on Transnational Corporations, *Report on the Fourth Session*, E/C. 10/43 (1978), p. 27.

20. United Nations, *The impact of Multinational Corporations on Development and on International Relations*, ST/ESA/6 (1974).

Chapter Three

TRENDS, DETERMINANTS AND IMPACT OF THE ACTIVITIES OF TRANSNATIONAL ENTERPRISES

Changing economic and socio-political conditions have affected the activities of TNEs. It is the purpose of this chapter to assess the past and present trends, determinants, and different impacts of the activities of TNEs and of foreign direct investment in general. On this basis, it will be possible to better understand the differences in national policies and the international approaches regarding direct investment and to consider later on the future role to be played by TNEs in a new international economic system.

1. Trends

1.1. *Magnitude and growth*

Direct investment occured on a relatively modest scale prior to World War I. The capital transfers, emanating mainly from Europe (particularly the United Kingdom) and the United States, and destined largely for Latin America and overseas colonies, most frequently took the form of portfolio lending by private lenders to both public and private borrowers. The purpose of much of this investment was to develop the production of foodstuffs and raw materials; these investments were supplemented by substantial investment in railways, public utilities and the like, to provide required infrastructure.[1]

Concerning direct investment in manufacturing, some impression is given by the figures for a sample of 187 U.S.-controlled TNEs. In 1900, these enterprises had 47 manufacturing subsidiaries, including three in countries that now are classified as developing countries. Since 1900 this form of investment has, of course, increased enormously in both absolute and relative importance (Table 1).

Table 1. *Number of foreign manufacturing subsidiaries of 187 U.S.-controlled manufacturing enterprises, selected years, 1900-1967*

	Total	Latin America	Other[a]
1900	47	3	0
1913	116	10	1
1919	180	20	7
1929	467	56	23
1939	715	114	28
1950	988	259	42
1959	1,891	572	128
1967	3,646	950	454
1970	6,439	1,489	821
1973	8,945	2,134	1,265
1975	11,122	2,770	1,741

[a]Other than Europe, Canada, Latin America and the Southern Dominions. Source: Vaupel and Curhan, *The Making of Multinational Enterprises*, 1969; and Curhan, Davidson and Suri, *Tracing the Multinationals*, 1977.

The most rapid periods of growth were immediately before World War I, during the 1920s, after 1950 and, in particular, between 1967 and 1973. Over the period shown, the number of manufacturing subsidiaries located in the developing countries increased from a very small proportion to about two-fifths.

Data on the value of direct investment over the years are sketchy and incomplete. Figures for the U.S., where investors have traditionally been particularly active in this area, indicate that in 1929 the book value of foreign direct investment in manufacturing subsidiaries of U.S. firms totalled $1.8 billion; by 1940 this figure had grown to $3.8 billion; by 1957 to $8.0 billion; by 1967 to $56.6 billion; by 1973 to $101.3 billion; and, by 1976 to $137.2 billion.[2]

TNEs, therefore, have continued to expand in the 1970s. The number of enterprises that can be considered transnational is substantial. If all firms with at least one foreign affiliate are included, some 10,000 have been identified in 1973.[3] Of this total number of firms, which are drawn from all sectors, nearly 45 per cent had affiliates in only one foreign country, while less than 4 per cent had affiliates in more than 20 countries. The latter are heavily concentrated in a few home countries, such as the United States, Japan, the United Kingdom, the Federal Republic of Germany, the Netherlands, Sweden and Switzerland.[4]

The total sales of foreign affiliates (excluding intra-firm sales) of all industrial firms with at least one foreign affiliate is estimated to have been about $670 billion in 1976.[5] The corresponding figure for industrial firms with consolidated sales of $1 billion or more is estimated to be about $410 billion in the same year. Available evidence indicates, however, that the relative importance of large enterprises in total foreign sales declined in the 1970s.[6] Although these figures are not exactly comparable, they give some indication of the relative importance of the world's largest firms.

Another possible measure of the growth of TNEs in recent years is the estimated 80 per cent increase (in current dollars) in the stock of foreign direct investment from $158 billion in 1971 to $287 billion in 1976 (Table 2). However, since the first half of the 1970s was a period of considerable inflation and in particular of a progressive weakening of the U.S. dollar relative to the currencies of several major countries of origin of direct investment, the figures on the direct investment stock do not reflect the real magnitude. For that reason it might be useful to compare the increase in the direct investment stock with that of the combined gross national product (GNP) of the developed market economies (where all but a small fraction of direct investment originates). This comparison shows that stocks of direct investment have grown at roughly the same as the GNP of developed countries (Table 3). But this still tells only part of the story, because the expansion has involved an increased use of nonequity arrangements such as franchising, licensing and management contracts, as many host countries — in particular developing ones — favour such arrangements as they provide a means of acquiring the skills and products developed by the TNE without creating a long-staying foreign-owned entity within their borders. In this context the continued expansion of TNE activities in socialist countries must be mentioned. These activities regularly also take the form on nonequity arrangements referred to as industrial cooperation.[7]

Table 2. *Stock of direct investment abroad of developed market economies, by major country of origin, 1967-1976*

Country of origin	Billions of dollars, end of				
	1967	1971	1974	1975	1976
United States	56.6	82.8	101.3	124.2	137.2
United Kingdom	17.5	23.7	26.9	30.8	32.1
Germany, Fed. Rep.	3.0	7.3	11.9	16.0	19.9
Japan	1.5	4.4	10.3	15.9	19.4
Switzerland	5.0	9.5	11.1	16.9	18.6
France	6.0	7.3	8.8	11.1	11.9
Canada	3.7	6.5	7.8	10.5	11.1
Netherlands	2.2	4.0	5.5	8.5	9.8
Sweden	1.7	2.4	3.0	4.4	5.0
Belgium-Luxembourg	2.0	2.4	2.7	3.2	3.6
Italy	2.1	3.0	3.2	3.3	2.9
Total above	101.3	153.3	192.5	243.8	270.4
All other (estimate)	4.0	5.1	6.3	15.1	16.8
Grand total	105.3	158.4	298.8	258.9	287.2

Source: U.N. ECOSOC Commission on Transnational Corporations, *Transnational Corporations in World Development: A Re-examination*, E/C.10/38 (1978), p. 236.

Table 3. *Comparison of increase in direct investment stock with combined GNP of DAC countries*

	1967	1971	1976	1967-71	1971-76
Item	Billions of current U.S. dollars			Average annual rate of increase (percentage)	
1. GNP of DAC countries	1 561,4	2 213,1	4 167	9.1	13.5
2. Direct investment stock	105,2	158,1	287,4	10.7	12.7
3. Ratio 2./1. (per cent)	6.7	7.1	6.9		

Source: OECD, *Development Cooperation* (various years, 1967-1976); OECD, *Penetration of Multinational Enterprises in Manufacturing Industry in Member Countries*, 1977.

1.2. *Sectoral distribution*

The major share of foreign direct investment has long been and remains in the manufacturing sector. Very roughly one quarter of the assets of TNEs is in extractive industries, one quarter in services of all types, and one half in manufacturing. Table 4 gives an impression of the stock of direct investment abroad by major industrial sectors — total and in developing countries — for four selected developed market economies. The Table shows that service industries, including, in particular, banking and insurance, have experienced pronounced international growth rates. In the raw material industries, investments from Japan and the Federal Republic of Germany have expanded, offsetting a United States and United Kingdom slowdown, which was partly due to nationalisation. As to the manufacturing sector, it might be noted that high technology industries continue to show signs of faster international growth than others.[8]

As far as foreign direct investment in the OECD countries is concerned, the growth rates in the service sector may be explained by the results obtained in numerous cross-section analyses, which have shown that the share of industrial production in the GNP tends to increase with growing per capita incomes up to a certain critical income level. After this level has been achieved the share of industrial production in GNP declines in favour of a substantial expansion of the service sector.[9] Most of the major industrialised market economies have now passed over that turning point, though the achievement of the turning point has been sometimes delayed by granting direct subsidies to the industries concerned or by an undervaluation of the specific country's currency.[10]

Growth of foreign direct investment in the service sector in the developing countries may have different reasons: firms tend to develop exports and trade-related services abroad before establishing manufacturing operations outside their home countries. In other instances, service firms have been pulled abroad by the prior expansion of their clients.[11]

1.3. *Developing countries' share in foreign direct investment*

At the end of 1970 the book value of the private foreign direct investment located in developing countries totalled approximately $40 billion. This represents roughly a quarter of the total stock of direct investment in the world. Direct investment enterprises accounted for some 6 per cent of the total output in the developing countries. Compared to the total stock of capital and the total level of output, foreign direct investment has been more important for the developing countries as a group than for developed countries. This is true not only in extractive industries, where foreign investment has been of considerable significance but also in the manufacturing sector. Comparing the stock of direct investment at the end of 1970 to GNP in 1970, one finds a ratio of 0.090 for all developing countries and about 0.059 for developed countries.[12]

Table 4. *Selected developed market economies; stock of direct investment abroad by major industrial sector, total and in developing countries, 1971 and latest available year (in millions of dollars)*

Country and industrial sector	Total stock		Stock in developing countries	
	1971[a]	1974[a]	1971[a]	1974[a]
United States				
Extractive[b]	30 989,2	36 771,3	8 339,2	5 191,4
Manufacturing	44 370,1	61 062,1	7 820,4	11 362,3
Services	25 954,3	39 411,1	6 745,2	12 497,2
United Kingdom[c]				
Extractive	8 051,2	8 747,1	1 159,4[d]	989,2[d]
Manufacturing	10 043,2	14 131,3	1 828,1	2 409,1
Services	5 633,1	8 399,3	1 524,4	1 661,4
Germany, Fed. Rep.				
Extractive	350,4	1 419,2	92,3	569,2
Manufacturing	5 796,2	14 032,3	1 605,3	3 633,1
Services	1 131,3	4 464,4	347,4	1 813,2
Japan				
Extractive	892,0	2 778,2	...	1 362,4
Manufacturing	1 092,0	3 723,4	...	2 887,3
Services	1 978,3	4 119,2	...	1 429,0

Source: As for Table 3.

a   Years for U.S. are 1973 and 1976; for Fed. Rep. of Germany, 1971 and 1976.

b   Refers to mining and smelting and petroleum.

c   Relevant sectoral stock data include investment in petroleum and insurance not included in the items for developing countries.

d   Refers to agriculture and petroleum only.

In the 1970s, TNEs have continued to concentrate their foreign activities in the developed market economies, which still account for nearly three-quarters of the total. Four countries —

Canada, the United States of America, the United Kingdom, and the Federal Republic of Germany — are host to 40 per cent of the total direct investment stock. The developing countries' share has declined in recent years. Table 5 gives an impression of the developing countries' share in foreign direct investment from three major capital-exporting countries.

As to the notion "developing countries," it is, of course, recognised in this study that, despite similarities of situation and a feeling of solidarity that goes beyond immediate short-term interests, the developing countries form a very heterogeneous group, whether in respect of per capita income (ranging from $110 in Bangladesh to $2,700 in Singapore in 1974-76), industrialisation (four countries — Argentina, Mexico, Brazil and India — among them accounted for 50 per cent of the entire Third World's industrial output in 1973), natural resources, or size of population.

Table 5. *The developing countries' share in foreign direct investment from major capital-exporting countries, 1960-1975 (per cent)*

Year	United States	United Kingdom	Fed. Rep. of Germany
1960	36.8	36.8	36.9
1962	34.1	37.4	36.8
1964	31.4	34.9	31.8
1966	29.4	31.7	30.4
1968	26.7	29.9	29.2
1970	25.4	28.9	29.4
1972	25.3	26.3	29.6
1974	24.0	..	29.4
1975	..	..	29.3

Source: Krägenau, Internationale Direktinvestitionen, 1975.

Within the group of developing countries the activities of TNEs are heavily concentrated in a few of the larger, more industrial-

ised countries and in those possessing important natural resources: More than one-fifth of the direct investment stock in
developing countries in 1975 was held by oil-producing countries and a further two-fifths by 10 other countries. While the
amount available for the multitude of other developing countries was correspondingly reduced, the share of foreign enterprises in the respective local economies may, as has been noted
already, nevertheless be substantial from the point of view of
some host developing countries. Frequently it is quite large in
the extractive sector and in the relatively small modern manufacturing sector.[13] The relative importance of direct investment
thus varies enormously from host developing country to host
developing country. The fact, however, that the smaller, poorer
countries have attracted a declining share of TNE assets suggests
that these enterprises play only a rather limited role in fulfilling
the needs of pre-industrial societies. The implications of this
observation will be further explored in Chapter Six below.

The situation is quite different in the more advanced developing countries. According to an EEC study,[14] the developing
countries where the TNEs are more frequently represented are
Brazil (1, 612 TNEs foreign ventures, i.e. 8 per cent of the total
number of TNEs foreign ventures), Mexico (1, 402, i.e. 6.9 per
cent), Argentina (890, i.e. 4.4 per cent), India (716, i.e. 3.5 per
cent), Singapore (703, i.e. 3.4 per cent), Malaysia (654, i.e. 3.2
per cent), and Venezuela (631, i.e. 3.1 per cent).

The general network of interconnections created by TNEs'
investments between the developed market economies and the
developing countries is shown in Table 6. This Table calls for
several observations such as, for instance, the fact that the U.S.
appears as a base country for TNEs well behind the EEC, and
especially the United Kingdom, which appears to be by far the
most important base country for TNEs operating in the developing countries; however, this Table contains only the quantitative distribution of TNEs subsidiaries and does not give any information on the size of the operations. For our purpose, however, which is to determine the role to be played by the TNEs in
a new international economic system, the knowledge of this
North-South interconnection system is quite important. It helps

to identify the countries and zones of the developing countries for which the perspective of further development of manufacturing appears to be most likely because significant industrial development is already underway. It is also worth noticing that a few developing countries appear themselves to be base countries for TNEs — such as, besides India, Brazil and Venezuela, the cases of Malaysia, Singapore, Hong Kong. This aspect may be worth attention, since it casts some new and unusual light on the integration of the industrial structures of developing countries and developed market economies.

1.4. *Intra-firm transactions*

With the expansion of TNE operations intra-firm transactions have assumed a great importance in world trade. Although information is limited, studies show, for example, that about half the United States exports and imports at the beginning of the 1970s represented intra-firm dealings and recent data suggest a further upswing.[15] Greater intra-firm flows have indeed important managerial consequences. The most important of these is that in order to maintain control of the complex flows of goods among the various subsidiaries and subunits in different countries, TNEs need to exert a degree of control at a level in the hierarchy above that of the national subsidiary. As the enterprises have generally developed standard procedures for production and sale, centralizing tendencies may be exercised more by the harmonisation of functions than by direct central authority. Thus, the more national units become conditioned to indirect harmonized control procedures, the more difficult it may become for them to respond to the needs of the local economy.[16] These centralising pressures, operating to a large degree in the manufacturing TNEs, are felt also in the banks, advertising agencies, consultancies and other industries in the service sector.[17]

Within many sectors the growing trend is one of tightening interdependence within TNEs, just as can be perceived for the economies in general. It must, of course, again be noted that the forces at work focus on some regions within the developed

Table 6. *Distribution of "TNE's Subsidiaries in the LDC's"*[a]

	France	Belgium	Netherlands	Germany	Italy	U.K.	Ireland	Denmark	Luxembourg	Total EEC
Algeria	117	–	5	8	3	3	–	–	1	137
Argentina	80	21	18	116	29	130	–	3	6	403
Bahamas	9	9	6	11	8	191	–	3	2	239
Barbados	–	–	–	1	–	36	–	–	–	37
Brazil	108	35	50	280	52	183	–	18	10	736
Cameroun	101	2	6	5	4	8	–	–	2	132
Chile	17	9	6	33	5	40	–	–	1	111
Columbia	17	9	18	26	21	22	–	4	1	118
Congo	45	117	2	3	6	5	–	–	4	182
Costa Rica	2	–	4	1	68	–	–	–	–	75
Cyprus	2	2	7	–	–	58	1	–	1	71
Ecuador	3	4	2	7	6	27	–	–	–	49
El Salvador	1	–	6	5	–	9	–	–	–	21
Ethiopia	9	–	3	5	18	12	–	1	2	50
Fiji	–	2	–	2	–	26	–	1	2	33
Gabon	39	2	9	3	2	10	–	–	–	65
Ghana	3	1	7	12	2	81	–	–	–	106
Guatemala	–	–	4	10	1	5	–	–	–	20
Guyana	1	–	1	1	–	48	–	1	–	52
India	17	9	17	91	4	341	–	5	–	485
Indonesia	2	–	16	16	1	51	–	6	2	110
Iran	17	4	12	53	6	39	–	3	–	139
Israel	6	–	1	12	–	22	–	3	–	44
Ivory Coast	105	4	11	15	4	15	–	–	2	156
Jamaica	1	–	3	3	–	107	–	–	3	117
Kenya	4	1	14	19	4	391	–	7	–	440
Lebanon	14	2	6	9	4	24	–	–	–	59
Liberia	19	–	8	10	5	23	–	–	–	65
Malagasy Rep.	69	–	9	7	4	6	–	–	–	95
Malaysia	6	5	22	11	2	313	–	5	1	369
Malawi	1	2	2	6	–	85	–	4	–	100
Malta	–	–	3	–	3	73	–	–	2	81
Mexico	45	11	17	104	22	83	–	2	–	285
Morocco	274	20	12	27	15	22	–	2	5	377
Nicaragua	–	–	4	1	–	4	–	–	–	9
Nigeria	24	2	21	44	11	325	–	2	–	430
Pakistan	3	–	7	21	–	73	–	1	1	104
Panama	13	10	5	13	5	42	–	–	1	88
Peru	11	9	15	22	19	39	–	3	1	119
Philippines	–	–	6	7	–	18	–	3	–	34
Senegal	82	2	7	3	3	11	–	–	1	109
Singapore	7	–	25	38	4	270	–	1	1	346
South Africa	62	20	80	256	8	2,516	1	25	3	2,971
South Korea	–	–	3	7	–	4	–	–	–	14
Sri Lanka	–	–	2	3	–	69	–	3	–	77
Tanzania	1	–	8	10	2	93	–	1	–	115
Thailand	2	1	20	20	1	60	–	11	–	115
Trinidad and Tobago	–	–	3	4	1	83	–	1	–	92
Tunisia	59	6	10	4	7	9	–	–	1	96
Turkey	13	–	11	37	16	21	–	3	2	105
Uganda	1	1	5	6	1	123	–	3	–	139
Uruguay	9	8	1	4	6	16	–	–	1	45
Venezuela	28	18	33	37	16	52	–	5	1	192
Zaire	37	223	18	12	5	43	–	–	14	357
Zambia	1	2	7	1	3	228	–	1	–	243
Other Countries	172	44	56	60	38	259	–	18	1	647
TOTAL	1,658	633	656	1,531	379	6,921	2	149	77	12,006

[a] UNCTAD Members: Industrialized Countries (ICs) with more than 80 subsidiaries in LDCs.
LDCs with more than 50 subsidiaries from ICs.

Norway	Sweden	Switzer-land	USA	Canada	Malaysia	Singa-pore	Japan	Hong Kong	Austra-lia	Other	TOTAL
1	2	3	12	–	–	–	–	–	1	2	158
4	68	48	332	11	–	–	10	–	14	14	890
–	1	18	234	78	–	–	2	5	7	12	596
2	2	–	13	8	–	–	–	–	–	–	162
17	95	54	501	39	–	–	32	1	3	34	1,612
..	–	1	4	–	–	–	–	–	–	–	139
3	20	5	65	–	–	–	4	–	–	1	209
3	49	13	181	1	–	–	2	–	1	5	373
–	2	2	4	–	–	–	–	–	–	2	194
–	–	16	62	–	–	–	5	–	–	2	160
–	1	–	6	–	–	–	–	1	1	2	82
–	4	2	63	–	–	–	1	–	–	2	121
–	–	–	23	2	6	–	6	–	–	–	152
3	..	–	3	–	–	–	3	–	–	–	59
–	–	–	2	–	–	3	1	6	45	25	115
–	..	–	6	–	–	–	–	–	–	–	71
3	–	3	19	1	–	–	–	–	–	5	137
–	–	1	66	5	–	–	3	–	–	2	97
2	2	–	3	2	–	–	–	–	–	2	61
2	31	19	154	4	–	–	11	1	5	4	716
1	3	2	55	2	6	2	21	4	20	–	220
–	4	1	68	–	–	–	15	1	–	11	239
–	–	3	125	–	–	–	–	–	3	1	176
..	1	3	11	–	–	–	–	–	–	–	171
–	2	3	68	17	–	–	–	–	–	–	207
2	7	2	36	2	–	2	4	–	–	–	496
–	7	10	34	2	–	–	3	1	–	–	116
–	5	4	119	–	–	–	–	–	–	5	198
–	–	2	3	–	–	–	1	–	–	–	101
5	11	4	54	5	43	82	19	20	40	2	654
1	3	–	4	–	–	1	1	–	1	2	113
–	–	1	7	1	–	–	–	–	–	–	50
5	56	48	955	20	–	–	21	–	2	10	1,402
2	18	8	37	–	–	–	3	1	2	7	456
–	–	–	41	1	–	–	1	–	–	1	53
2	–	11	68	2	2	1	6	–	1	4	527
–	7	3	32	–	–	–	2	–	1	1	150
1	9	24	224	6	–	–	8	1	3	3	367
7	25	22	157	–	–	–	16	–	1	8	355
1	15	5	170	–	–	–	14	1	3	19	265
–	–	3	43	–	–	–	–	–	–	–	116
7	9	10	84	1	29	108	29	30	48	2	703
11	40	63	400	35	–	–	1	1	40	10	3,572
–	–	2	41	–	–	–	12	1	1	–	71
–	3	1	6	–	–	1	2	–	–	–	–
1	1	–	6	–	–	–	1	–	–	–	124
4	–	6	82	1	1	3	70	16	1	10	309
2	4	–	23	9	–	–	2	–	–	–	138
–	4	4	15	–	–	–	–	–	–	1	120
–	12	9	40	2	–	–	–	–	–	10	176
2	2	...	10	2	–	–	–	–	–	1	156
4	15	4	37	1	–	–	–	–	–	2	–
2	18	14	373	17	–	–	11	–	1	2	630
–	5	2	11	2	–	–	8	–	–	5	390
–	8	–	35	–	–	1	1	–	2	4	294
5	23	19	220	14	1	–	14	5	1	15	968
105	594	478	5,412	214	32	307	466	134	236	315	20,222

Source: Etude sur les entreprises multinationales, EEC Commission, March 1976.

market economies. The results produced by these forces may, however, also be felt in the more advanced developing regions of the world.

1.5. *Subcontracting*

The two main lines of interconnections that TNEs may establish when setting up their plants in developing countries are the flow of technological and managerial know-how towards the respective developing countries and the network of subcontracting arrangements. An important difference among the various branches engaged in subcontracting is the ownership of the local firm. Depending upon the economic advancement of the host country and the specific commercial activities of the enterprise, subcontracting takes place, both with locally owned firms and between the locally established plant and the plants in the base country.

In a few technologically less complex fields, subcontracting with locally owned firms is used increasingly. Such contracting arrangements may be accompanied by cooperation agreements in the field of management and technology. This alternative to the "classical" direct investment, though it is still one of dependence, may become more important in the future.

1.6. *New entrants and competition*

International operations are by no means the exclusive preserve of the giant corporations. There are signs that small TNEs are becoming increasingly active. There exist, for instance, a large number of small and medium-sized firms in the United States of America having significant foreign networks.[18] Also the large number of firms with at least one foreign affiliate, which have been referred to above,[19] reinforce the point. In addition to this increase in the relative importance of foreign investors from non-traditional sources, enterprises in some of the economically more important developing countries (see notably the countries mentioned in Table 6) and in the socialist states (which are also not traditional home countries) have also started going abroad.

So far, such developments do not account for significant sums of money as compared to the world's stock of direct investment. Yet, the respective growth rates seem to be impressive.[20] Thus, regional investment within Latin America appears to have substantially increased in 1975 and 1976. Similar observations can be made for direct investment operations proceeding from Hong Kong and Singapore.[21] The other source of new entrants into a field traditionally dominated by TNEs from developed market economies are the socialist countries which have created a framework for industrial cooperation in the technical, scientific and production-oriented fields. One type of cooperation that has evolved from this recent development is trade cooperation through joint ventures set up in Western countries for promoting the sale of products originating in the socialist countries. The partners in these "joint ventures" usually are the state-owned trade organizations of the respective socialist country and a Western enterprise. A recent survey[22] indicates that at least 312 subsidiaries or branch enterprises had been established by the Union of Soviet Socialist Republics and 6 other socialist countries of Eastern Europe in 16 Western industrialised countries by the end of 1977. They were mainly located in the Federal Republic of Germany, the United Kingdom and France; only 16 were in the United States of America. The total capital of these 312 subsidiaries was estimated at over US $600 million.

The growing number of new entrants into the international market place increases the potential for competition between these new firms and established TNEs, thus also increasing the alternatives open to host governments and possibly ultimately strengthening their bargaining positions. On the other hand, many of the newcomers are smaller companies unencumbered by established networks of foreign activities and may thus — to the extent that their operations are not limited by the constraints of a pre-established central plan, as is the case for the TNEs originating from socialist countries — be more responsive to the needs of local economies and more inclined to accept the terms and conditions set by host countries.

Finally, it should be indicated at this stage that a new type of foreign direct investment has emerged. This is a result of the sudden massive oil price increases and the relatively low absorption capacity of certain oil-producing countries as, for instance, Saudi Arabia. While the capital flows from these countries into the OECD area have primarily been characterised by large placements in highly liquid financial assets (bank deposits, government marketable securities), i.e., flows of funds to the Euromarket and to a limited number of industrialised countries, direct investments have so far been rather marginal in the whole, though heavily concentrated in a few ("blue chip") countries where they have indeed given rise to some public concern. These foreign direct investments are to be considered a new type of direct-investment flow because they are not made by foreign enterprises but by governments, they are not combined with a transfer of technology or managerial skills, and they concentrate almost exclusively on take-over operations. These characteristics set them apart from the type of investments which form the main subject of this study.

2. Determinants of direct investment

During the past two decades, the search for world-wide integrated operations may have been the principal reason why major TNEs have spread, i.e., the need to plan, organise and manage on a scale appropriate to the magnitude of technical and managerial resources required for modern technology, low cost production, and mass distribution. Another major reason for investing abroad was to ensure the access to raw materials. West European and Japanese TNEs were increasingly following the 1950-70 American trend of "going transnational" — i.e., exporting manufacturing business, rather than manufactured goods, to the outside world or undertaking appropriate contractual arrangements.

2.1. *Reasons for investing abroad*

The most often cited reasons for the growth of TNE activities and international direct investment, which naturally apply with different force to different parts of the world, are: (*i*) to gain access to cheaper labour and energy, as well as to escape in certain cases strict regulations and standards, e.g., against pollution; (*ii*) to take advantage of changing trade relations (this factor was especially important in the early 1960s) with the formation of the EEC, which American businessmen feared might effectively exclude their products); (*iii*) to get close to a growing foreign market (to save on transportation costs and enhance sensitivity to local market conditions); (*iv*) to prevent competitors from pre-empting a foreign market or source of supply (this motivation seems to be particularly conspicuous in the extraction of raw materials, advanced technology industries and banking, law and insurance); (*v*) to escape domestic anti-trust laws (during the 1960s some American investment took place abroad simply because anti-trust laws inhibited some of the biggest firms from investing at home; the EEC anti-trust policy may, on the other hand, be expected to be strengthened and to move part way towards the American system); (*vi*) to shield a big TNE from cyclical fluctuations in its home market (until 1974 trade cycles were generally not synchronised; thus market declines in profits at home could be offset by satisfactory earnings abroad); (*vii*) to obtain the advantages of more thoroughly integrated operations on a large scale (it has already been said that this may have been the principal reason why TNEs have spread; the computer led revolution is possibly going to make those advantages of integrated operations more important still); (*viii*) to secure raw material sources.

It is apparent that these various hypotheses are by no means mutually exclusive but are interrelated; there is no reason to believe that there is one unique determinant of foreign investment. In terms of the usual discount equation[23] designed to evaluate the relative attractiveness of investing abroad as compared to investing at home, each of the hypotheses mentioned above point to a factor that is important in altering one or more of the terms on the right-hand side of the equation and thereby having an important effect on the net present value of the investment. Investors, given these determinants of investment and a range of investment outlets in a variety of countries, may be viewed as attempting to allocate an optimal stock of their capital to each use and to each country. A change in one variable in one country may be expected to induce a reallocation of investment in not only a particular activity taking place in one country but also in other activities and in other countries as the investor normally attempts to regain an optimal (profit-maximising) allocation of his resources in the face of a change in the factors affecting the return on his investment;[24] because — to restate a platitude which nonetheless underlines an important point — private foreign investment is undertaken for purpose of making a private profit; and as, compared to domestic investment, foreign direct investment is rather complex and risky, a premium over what can be earned at home may frequently be required to induce investors to undertake investment abroad.

The main cause for international investment (in the classical form of control or in the form of contracting arrangements) may hence be a willingness to increase profits by taking advantage of some technological or managerial superiority or distinctiveness, or an attempt to lower the relative costs of various factors of production and to secure particular factor endowments, or the objective of strengthening the market position or entering new markets.

In the field of manufacturing the direct investor sometimes attempts to exploit a new innovation under monopolistic market conditions. The most important industries engaging in direct investments, indeed, used to be those where monopolistic market conditions prevailed. The automobile industry and the computer industry are typical examples; these are areas in which size and advanced technology play a large role and where the scope for innovations is large; these innovations and benefits of extensive research can then be applied by the direct investor from a strong market position.

There are additional and more specific reasons which might determine an enterprise to invest abroad, such as, in particular, incentive policies pursued by home and host countries. Incentives raise important questions from the standpoints of both the effect on the supply of foreign investment and the benefits derived therefrom by the host country. Such incentives arrangements are exceedingly complex and differ greatly among host countries and in particular among developing countries.

A review of the nature and extent of incentive measures pursued by home and host countries will be undertaken in Chapter Four. What matters at the present stage of the study is the question of the extent to which these incentives affect the TNEs decisions about where to locate projects. Evidence based on the responses of business firms to question about the effect of incentives in their investment decisions lead to the conclusion that incentives are indeed of some importance, particularly those provided via trade policy and tax measures; on the other hand, most enterprises are aware of the difficulties posed by such incentives and frequently assert that they are reluctant to undertake projects that are heavily dependent for their success upon incentives provided by the host country, as the long-term future of the project may, for obvious reasons, be subject to some risk. This in turn may set some limits to the incentive system.

2.2. *"Disincentives" — political investment risks*

There exist "disincentives" to foreign direct investment, i.e., there are measures in the field of direct investment regulation, taxation, interest rates or in other areas, which are specifically designed to discourage foreign direct investment; but there are also policies, attitudes, anticipated political and economic developments which (indirectly) may have the collateral effect of an investment disincentive and thus discourage foreign investors from investing. For instance, the prospects for foreign direct investment in the developing countries are sometimes distorted by certain non-economic factors, notably by political investment risks.

Capital flows to developing countries have been and still are distored by various events, such as, in particular, a possibly increasing propensity in certain countries to expropriate TNEs without fair compensation, to impose controls on TNEs, to provide joint venture regulations and/or "fade-out-investment" schemes, and to exclude the possibility that, in case of conflicts with the host government, an investor may appeal to international law and/or international courts of justice. In addition, the over-proportional political instability of most of the developing countries prevents investors from trusting in host countries' investment laws and guarantee declarations.

Bilateral agreements on the protection of foreign investment which have been settled between most of the developed countries and many developing countries may be helpful. On the other hand, their value may be questionable for a number of reasons: they do not, in fact, allow for substantial guarantees; the developing countries involved normally never bind themselves to not expropriating foreign investment; the Latin American developing countries in many cases do not agree upon investment treaties; and the agreements so far concluded do not result in a homogeneous international investment framework which would be relevant for multinational investment projects. Thus, as empirically shown in a recent enquiry, bilateral investment treaties in practice seem to be of comparatively reduced significance either as an incentive or as a protective measure.[25] Of much greater relevance are, on the other hand, the governmental guarantee and insurance systems related to such investment agreements.

The simplest way to project an investment against investment risks is, of course, not to invest at all. As such an attitude on principle does not make sense from an economic point of view, a rational investor has to weigh risk and profit expectations and to balance one against the other.[26] Whenever an investor must decide whether or not he is prepared to invest in a developing country, apart from other investment determinants, he has to assess the specific investment climate; i.e., he will have to find out or to guess whether the respective host country is likely to change its present investment conditions and the extent to which such a change would affect his profit expectations. However, in most cases reliable information about future developments is not at hand; it might be provided by extrapolating past and present trends, but this usually implies difficult and expensive data gathering. Another method, therefore, might consist in the development of indicators for a country's political stability and investment climate. Such indicators have been developed.[27] Their utilisation must, however, be subject to considerable limitations and complemented by carefully observing the current situation. As the predictive power of such indices is, in fact, not too great, they may be used only as a "rule of thumb". But, taking these limitations into account, such indices might serve as a first approximation for business environmental analysis and thus allow the investor to avoid those investments where risk is comparatively high.

2.3. *Common patterns*

Evidence[28] suggests that despite the variety of influences affecting direct investment in the developing countries, a number of common patterns allowing for an answer to the question, "why do enterprises invest in the developing countries?". may be identified, bearing in mind that the characteristics and determinants of direct investment appear to differ considerably depending on the type of investment. First, the current rate of profit, measured on an accounting basis, appears to have little or no relation to the level of investment; at the same time, however, there is little doubt that prospective profit over the life of investments has a basic influence on the level of investments; i.e., the investor will always try to achieve an optimal allocation of his resources. Second, to some extent, the level of investment appears to be influenced by liquidity considerations − not so much the overall liquidity of the investing firm but the internal cash flows emanating from existing investments in the developing countries and perhaps also by the liquidity of local firms that may be taken over through foreign investment. Finally, the most important determinants of direct investment in the developing countries appear to be a variety of longer-term strategic considerations also related in particular to long-term profitability, market size and potential. Longer-term strategic factors are, e.g., the desire to gain and maintain a foothold in a protected market or to gain and maintain a low-cost source of supply, the desire to induce a host country into a long-run commitment to a particular type of technology, competition for market shares among oligopolists, and the economies of product-differentiated oligopoly — all considerations with longer-term and wider manifestations than the rate of return on investment as it is narrowly defined.

As to product differentiation and oligopoly, the most important industries engaging in direct investments are, as already explained, indeed those where "quasi-monopolistic" market conditions prevail. The automobile industry, the pharmaceutical industry, the petroleum industry, and the computer industry are typical examples; these are areas in which size and advanced technology play a large role and where the scope for innovations, both technological and managerial, is large. Big enterprises can indeed support more extensive research programmes and the benefits of the research can be applied from a commanding market position.[29] The direct investor thus may begin from a position of some monopoly power at home and arrive at a monopolistic position abroad. The fact that, typically, in forcing direct investment, the enterprise is trying to exploit a new innovation under monopolistic market conditions also helps to explain why certain TNEs are, in practice, not in favour of partnerships or joint ventures.

The emphasis on the longer-term aspects also implies that direct investment may not be particularly sensitive to short-run variations in liquidity, profits, output, or minor changes in policies vis-à-vis taxes and subsidies. Direct investment may, however, be sensitive to changes in political or economic circumstances that basically change the longer-term outlook for the investor's operations.

The above considerations should not hide the present lack of attractiveness to TNEs of the least developed countries.[30] As has been noted earlier, TNEs — the majority of which is based in some of the major developed countries — have invested only about one-quarter of their foreign assets in developing countries and this proportion is now even more declining. In addition OPEC countries and the so-called tax havens hold over one-third of the total direct investment stock in developing countries and ten other countries are host to 40 per cent of that stock; concentration within this top ten has increased over the period

1967-1975.[31] Peter Drucker,[32] to a large extent, is still right in saying that, while in the first instance extractive industries have to go wherever the petroleum, copper ore, or bauxite is found, whether in developing or in a developed country, for the typical twentieth-century TNE (that is a manufacturing, distributing, or financial company), most of the developing countries are neither important as markets nor as producers of profits. Thus, while for the extractive industries some developing countries are of significance as sources of profits, loci of growth, or as areas of investment, contrary to the fashionable but too simplistic theory of "capitalist imperialism", developing countries are at present generally not major sources of sales, revenues, profits, and growth, because sales growth and profits are where the market and the purchasing power are.

To the developing countries, however, the TNEs are both highly important and highly visible; neglect and indifference rather than "exploitation" is the real and justified grievance of many developing countries in respect to the TNEs.

3. Impact — real and perceived

The views regarding foreign direct investment and the activities of TNEs are still polarized.

3.1. *Proponents*

The proponents of the TNE say:
—by focussing on economic rationality, the TNE represents the interests of all against the parochial interests of separate nations; it is the most effective counter to rampant nationalism and to a concept of sovereignty made obsolescent by the intensity of our interdependence; the only political weapon of the TNE is that it can remove its benefits from countries that are confiscatorily anti-business;
—TNEs are breaking down market imperfections; under critical circumstances, they are an element of security and stability;
—foreign direct investment creates jobs in both capital import-

ing and exporting countries and boosts home country as well as host country growth;
—the TNE is the best available mechanism to train people for modern managerial skills;
—no more effective instrument has been found for the diffusion of technology;
—the TNE is the most promising instrument for the transfer of capital (and appropriate technology) to the developing world, and its role will be crucial in overcoming the income gap which endangers world peace;
—the TNE's integrated and rationalised operations make it incomparably efficient; it provides to the consumer a better product at a lower cost; the TNE has proven its ability as an effective instrument for economic development;
—management of the TNEs is becoming increasingly flexible, sensitive to local custom and, in fact, genuinely international;
—the TNE reduces barriers to communications between people and establishes the basis for a stable world order.

3.2. *Critics*

The opposite views are held by the critics of the transnational enterprises:
—TNEs remove a significant part of the national economy from responsible political control; on the other hand, TNEs invade national sovereignty and frustrate economic policies;
—TNEs ignore the pricing mechanism and hence cartelise the world economy and foul the adjustment processes of the monetary system; the sheer size and scope of TNEs represent unfair competition to local enterprises; with rare exceptions, the subsidiary does not export to its country of origin in order to avoid competing with its parent company and causing trouble with its labour force at home;
—while some believe that TNEs undermine the economy of the home country, others believe that it bleeds the host country to the benefit of the home country;
—TNEs do not train people in entrepreneurial skills, which is what a developing country needs more than executive skills;

—the transfer of technology is often minimised because (*a*) R & D is generally carried out by the parent company, (*b*) the training of nationals of the host country for R & D posts is often neglected, (*c*) the technology itself is often closely held;

—the cost of capital brought by the TNE is far higher than the host country would be charged as direct borrower in capital markets; the transnational enterprise often invests relatively little of its own capital and manages to buy up domestic enterprises with local capital. The profits of the TNEs are exorbitantly high and too low a proportion of them are reinvested;

—the TNE often distorts development programs by channelling its reported profits to countries where taxation is lowest by manipulating charges for services and transactions on behalf of particular affiliates so as to disguise real earnings in high tax countries ("transfer pricing"); TNEs organise their affairs in such a way that excessive parts of profits of the group accrue to an affiliated company established in a country where company taxation is low or nil ("use of tax havens");

—since the strength of the TNE lies in integrated operations and centralised control, the intersets of the parent company must remain dominant and the TNE cannot ever become genuinely international; often the TNE resists genuine internationalisation by declining (*a*) to put foreigners into management and (*b*) to make shares of affiliates available to nationals of the host country;

—regarding industrial relations, critics of the TNE stress the following issues: union recognition, formal as distinct from real compliance with rules governing worker representation, different dismissal procedures, non-compliance with local norms in the determination of wages and conditions of work, the ability to switch production to another country in the face of strike action, difficulties in identifying locus of decision-making for purposes of collective bargaining.

3.3. *Benefits and costs*

There exist, in addition, numerous other conflicting views about the effects of foreign investment on host countries, especially in relation to the particular situation in the Third World, concerning, e.g., "corrupt practices and illicit payments" or the issues relating to the so-called "brain drain" from developing to developed countries.

There is also dispute about the outlook of these enterprises: Some see them "taking over the World" and supplanting nation-states as effective decision-making units, while others foresee a process of "dinosaurisation" through which their size both dulls their dynamics and compels governments to bring these enterprises firmly under their control.[33]

No attempt will be made here to analyse and confirm or rebut in detail all arguments and propositions advanced by the proponents and critics of TNE. Some of the criticism reflects real issues while other views advanced by the critics may primarily represent a problem of perception; some remarks invite extensive empirical research, other ask for an ideological discussion.

3.3.1. *Benefits for host countries—relocation*

Though the author of the study is aware that there are controversies about the desirability and real contribution of foreign direct investment to the development process of the developing countries, the study is founded on the basic idea that, in general, the promotion of direct investment in developing countries is a rational means to achieve higher welfare levels (indifference curves) in a certain group of developing countries as well as in the developed countries.

This statement is based neither on the developing countries' claim for more direct investment nor on the (normative) consideration that direct investment, by making a substantial contribution to developement in terms of transfer of technology, managerial and associated skills, increasing output, employment and strengthening of the balance-of-payments of the developing countries, may contribute to closing the depressing world-wide development gap between industrialised countries and developing countries. The above basic thesis is rather determined by the findings of international economic theory, i.e., the theory of the international division of labour between the various countries according to each country's specific comparative advantages.[34] The actual efficiency of the international division of labour in the field of production depends notably on the relocation of industrial production from industrialised countries to developing countries. International investment and TNE activities are an important aspect of the relocation process.

This movement is mainly due to the circumstance that, to a large extent, labour-intensive and/or raw material-intensive industrial production in certain sectors of the economies of the industrialised countries increasingly fail to be efficient and competitive because unskilled labour and raw material are scarce and/or expensive in the developed countries. Developing countries, however, are abundantly endowed with these factors, but not yet with capital and technology. Therefore, an international optimum of allocation (i.e., a substantial improvement in the international division of labour) could be achieved by relocating such industries to the developing countries; this might be done by enhancing the role of direct investment in the developing countries' manufacturing sector.

In fact, the competitiveness of the developed countries in certain parts of industrial production tends to drop because, for instance, an increased scarcity of environment leads to higher costs of production. In addition, the productivity of capital tends to decline due to the excess supply of capital in these countries. As indicated cross-section analyses have shown that the share of industrial production in GDP tends to increase with growing per capita incomes up to a certain critical income level; after that the tertiary sector begins to expand substantially and continuously unless advanced technologies such as microprocessors again revense this process.

Most of the developed countries may have passed that turning point by now. The present level of per capita incomes in developing countries is, on the other hand, still far away from this stage. Therefore, in the developing countries the share of industrial production in GDP can (and will) still increase.

In the face of these considerations, the developing countries' so-called "25 per cent target"[35] in principle does not appear utopian. This target is based on the developing countries' projection (UNIDO) that their share in world industrial production will rise from 7 per cent to at least 25 per cent by the year 2000.

It is certain that the 25 per cent target can be achieved only if the developing countries do not fail to be successful in attracting direct investment from the developed countries.[36] The following branches of the manufacturing sector, apart from raw material-intensive industries, could be identified as suitable for developing countries: clothing, leather products, musical instruments, toys, jewellery, sporting goods, shoes, wood products, plastic products, textiles, furniture, glass products, and some domestic electrical equipment.[37]

Thus it may be stated that, at least in the absence of any capital flow distortions (e.g., due to political investment risks), the flow of direct or alternative forms of investment to the developing countries might considerably expand in the future and increasingly concentrate on the developing countries' manufacturing sector.

The actually growing opposition from trade unions to relocation should not be forgotten here. Trade unions from industrialised countries are in a delicate position. They normally underline their sensitivity to the needs and problems of developing countries. On the other hand, they must react to the threat of structural adjustments in their own countries implying negative effects on employment. Under these circumstances, some trade union leaders argue, however, that the greatest benefits resulting from relocation and the ensuing necessities for structural adjustment are derived by the very advanced Third World countries and in particular the TNEs, while the benefits to the low income countries are negligible.

Thus the relocation process of which direct investment is a part responds to economic rationality and implies favourable effects for the developing economies. In addition to certain specific benefits attributed by the proponents of TNE activities to direct investment operations, the latter, in general, are supposed to lead to an increase in the stock of resources in the developing countries, resulting in higher employment, reductions in prices, and increased wages. Another beneficial effect is the direct tax collected on the profits earned by the foreign affiliate. Because of the international double taxation agreements and high rates of taxation in the north, TNEs have an incentive to report profits in the developing countries.

Given the complementarity between direct investment and other types of foreign capital transfers as, e.g., official development aid (ODA), and investment out of domestic resources, it is indeed likely that private direct investment adds to domestic employment, increases local wages and reduces local prices relative to what would otherwise be the case.

3.3.2. *Costs*

The developing countries' demands for changes in international patent laws and for codes of conduct for the transfer of technology and control over the activities of TNEs attempt to minimise the costs and to maximise the beneficial effects of international direct investment in favour of the developing countries. All technicalities aside, these demands have the objective of obtaining the know-how and capital of the West at a much lower price than the price paid under current conditions. The basic question, therefore, is whether the present price is justified, i.e., required to maintain an optimum level of capital formation and technological development in the longer run, or whether the TNEs are in a strong *monopoly* position and are thus extracting excessively high prices from developing countries.

There are, depending on the field of business, varying degrees of competition among TNEs, there are new entrants, and there is competition among TNEs and local firms.

On the other hand, there exist many instances where competition is insufficient and elements of monopoly exist. Besides the fact that market dominance is one of the determinants for foreign direct investment, quasi-monopolistic positions of TNEs may be a result of the situation in which the appearance of potential competitors is often accompanied by an increase in product differentiation. New entrants, therefore, do not in all cases mean that competition is increased.

As to the developing countries' requests for relocating of industries, it must be understood that the social cost of industrialisation is enormous: there is the initial cost of forcing (pre-industrial) societies to conform to the organisation and re-quirements of industrialised societies. Then there is the oper-ating cost, as an industrial society develops its own dynamic of ex-sessive urbanisation, environmental waste pollution and so forth.[38]

Like the benefits, the costs of foreign investment emanate from a variety of effects that are difficult to assess. In addition to some of the negative aspects (such as restrictive business practices and transfer pricing which may distort the allocation of resources and the division of tax revenues, or corrupt prac-tices and illicit payments which may be vehicles for siphoning away benefits), there might under certain circumstances also be the adverse effect that direct investment may have on the eco-nomic allocation of domestic resources; a wide range of policies have therefore been adopted in almost every country relating to subsidies, trade protection, regional development and so forth. Related to this, private foreign investment may conceivably entail unwanted distributive effects.

A number of developing countries that are short of capital and technological capabilities encourage the entry of developed countries' enterprises by providing, for instance, factory build-ings free of charge, development grants, tax holidays, and even tariffs protecting domestic production by TNEs against imports. This tends to accentuate the fact that many developing coun-tries experience a development of export of primary activities and manufactures oriented mainly towards industrialised coun-tries. Thus, it might be useful to recall in this context that of the 7.95 per cent which was the share of developing countries in world manufacured exports in 1974, only 24 per cent concern intra-developing country trade.

In many cases the particular sort of economic relationships between developing countries and the industrialised countries has produced special forms of segmentation processes and, thus, of dual economies in the developing countries: the part of the national industry geared to satisfaction of domestic demand is quite distinct from the "enclave" which is export-oriented (mainly towards developed countries). Many observers wonder, indeed, whether such a dichotomy hinders the achievement of a balanced industrial growth because of the difficulties in promoting technical and economic linkages between these two parts, each being tied to very different types of markets.

While the progressive and partial integration of under developed countries in the world economy and, at the same time, the internationalisation of financial capital through the formation of direct investment flows and repatriation of profits has certainly led to a number of positive effects, it should be clearly understood that the percentage of profits repatriated from developing countries can also be much higher than the share they receive as recipients of foreign investment (Table 7).

Table 7. *U.S. direct investment outflows, reinvested and repatriated earnings (not including direct investment receipt of fees and royalties $3 billion in 1974) (in billions of dollars).*

		1966	%	1970	%	1974	%
Total	Investment position	51,8	100	75,5	100	118,6	100
	Outflow	3,6	100	4,3	100	7,5	100
	Repatriated earnings	5,2	100	4,8	100	17,6	100
	Reinvested earnings	1,8	100	3,2	100	7,5	100
DCs	Investment position	13,9	25,8	19,2	25,4	28,5	24
	Outflow	0,5	13,8	0,98	22,8	1,7	22,6
	Repatriated earnings	1,97	37,8	2,3	47,9	12,5	71
	Reinvested earnings	0,43	23,8	0,6	18,7	1,6	21,3

Source: *Survey of Current Business,* 1975.

The integration of the developing countries' economies in the (capitalist) world economy is obviously partial. Although in many countries the TNEs have helped widen the variety of economic activities which are undertaken, they are working — when they are not export-oriented — for a local market which is still very small, because of the very unequal income distribution, not to mention the disparity between the consumption pattern they tend to promote (since it would in many cases not be cost-effective in terms of the TNEs strategy to develop products adapted to a mass of consumers unable to be responsive to stimulated demand) and the more "traditional" ones which perpetuate themselves.

This is one of the reasons for the criticism concerning the failure of TNEs to adapt to local needs, customs, and practices, to integrate more fully into the local communities of the host nations. Some authors use the notion of "truncated" enterprises for this phenomenon, alleging that, because of the tendency of many TNEs to move towards an increase in intra-group transactions the subsidiaries of TNEs are incomplete, because they do not assume all the functions of a normal company and thereby provide only limited benefits to the host country.

Thus, foreign direct investment is, like other elements in the present international economic system, a double-sided affair, having positive as well as negative aspects and implying costs and benefits. The major objective of policy makers and executives should, therefore, be to create conditions in which, as far as possible, the positive aspects prevail for all parties.

Closely connected with the issues pertaining to the real and perceived costs and benefits of direct investment is the question of advanced technologies and governmental mismanagement, i.e. the problem concerning the price that developing countries are prepared to pay in terms of accepting inferior economic returns in order to gain various non-economic objectives (such as starting mere prestige projects) to which a number of these countries attach priority. Appropriate "small" technologies are, on the other hand, often prevented by nationalistic attitudes.

How much nationalism might host countries be able to justify "purchasing" by foregoing real economic benefits? While the legitimate concern about national sovereignty is fully recognised, there are indeed cases where it seems to be quite difficult to understand the trade-offs, if any, between economic and non-economic costs and benefits. One example in this context is that of a watch assembly plant where the dollar cost of imported watch parts plus the dollars used to remit interest and profits abroad were greater than the dollars required to import the final watches.[39]

In fact, the ruling groups in most developing countries have a kind of religious belief in the "powers of technology". They do not realise that "inventions" simply remain gadgets when the socio-economic environment is not prepared to make use of them in economic production or in the process toward the improvement of the skills and knowledge of people. Every technique bears its "genetic code" relating it to the society which engendered it.[40] When a low income developing country buys, e.g., modern computer equipment, it does not enter into the "age of information," because most components of the equipment will be imported. The "data centre" will be manned by foreigners; once some nationals have been highly trained, they will usually make their careers in the TNE by running the centre and thus they will also join the brain drain.

To be fair, one should not put all the blame for this sort of mismanagement on the national decision makers, because they tend to equate modernisation with Westernisation and are encouraged in this attitude by Western business representatives who know how lucrative trade in technology is. In addition, there are, indeed, areas where developing countries need the most modern technology to solve their problems, e.g., in the fields of communications, education, and transport. On the other hand, it is too simplistic to accuse the TNEs without distinction in cases of clear mismanagement by governmental authorities.

To conclude this chapter, one might consider the observation that important criticism of TNEs is based not so much on the premise that foreign investment is bad, but that the real benefits derived from direct investment operations and TNE activities could be still greater. This is one major aspect of the following analysis of governmental policies.

Notes to chapter three

1. Vaupel and Curham, *The making of Multinational Enterprises*, 1969, chapter 3.

2. Based on U.S. Department of Commerce data, *Survey of Current Business* (various issues).

3. EEC Commission, *Survey of Multinational Enterprises*, vol. 1, 1976. Even this major survey was not fully comprehensive.

4. U.N. ECOSOC Commission on Transnational Corporations, *Transnational Corporations in World Development: A Re-examination*, E/C. 10/38 (1978), p. 75 and p. 212.

5. As to the difficulties concerning the methods of estimation, see U.N. ECOSOC Commission on Transnational Corporations, *Transnational Corporations in World Development*, op. cit., p. 35.

6. See U.N. ECOSOC Commission on Transnational Corporations, *Transnational Corporations in World Development*, op. cit., p. 35.

7. See United Nations Economic Commission for Europe (ECE), *Analytical Report on Industrial Cooperation among ECE countries*, E/ECE/844 (1973); McMillan, "East-West Industrial Cooperation" in U.S. Congress. Joint Economic Committee, *East European Economies Post-Helsinki: A Compendium of Papers* (1977), p. 1186; see also U.N. ECOSOC Commission on Transnational Corporations, *Transnational Corporations in World Development*, op. cit., p. 193 (Annex II); see also Levinson, *Vodka-Cola*, 1977 (annex with data and statistical material).

8. U.N. ECOSOC Commission on Transnational Corporations, *Transnational Corporations in World Development*, op. cit., p. 45.

9. Cf. Fels, Schatz and Wolter, "Der Zusammenhang zwischen Produktionsstruktur und Entwicklungsniveau," *Weltwirtschaftliches Archiv*, vol. 106, II (1971), p. 240.

10. As, for instance, in the case of the Deutsche mark up to the end of the 1960s.

11. See Bertin and Escaffre, *Internationalisation des grandes banques mondiales*, 1975; also, Steuber, *Internationale Banken: Auslandsaktivitäten von Banken bedeutender Industrieländer*, 1974.

12. See Reuber, *Private Foreign Investment in Development*, 1973, p. 4.

13. U.N. ECOSOC Commission on Transnational Corporations, *Transnational Corporations in World Development*, op. cit., p. 8. and 56.

14. EEC Commission, *Survey*, op. cit.

15. *The CTC Reporter*, vol. 1, no. 4 (1978), p. 3. Some TNEs have also developed extensive inter-affiliate trade patterns in third countries. In this context, see also U.S. Department of Commerce, *Foreign Direct Investment in the United States, Benchmark Survey*, 1974, 1976, vol. 2.

16. See Dunning and Gilman in Curzon, *Multinational Enterprises in a Hostile World*, 1977.

17. Cf., for instance, the review contained in Davis and Lawrence, *Matrix*, 1977, pp. 211-222.

18. See *Conference Board Report*, First Quarter, 1977.

19. EEC Commission, *Survey*, op. cit.

20. U.N. ECOSOC Commission on Transnational Corporations, *Transnational Corporations in World Development*, op. cit., p. 51.

21. To the extent that tax considerations have played a role, Hong Kong and Singapore are indirect investors of capital originating in developed market economies.

22. McMillan, "East-West industrial cooperation," op. cit.; U.N. ECOSOC Commission on Transnational Corporations, *Transnational Corporations in World Debelopment*, op. cit., p. 53.

23. The value of an investment from the investor's viewpoint may be thought of as being equal to the net present value of the expected future stream of net revenue emanating from the investment. One way of describing this is as follows:

$$NVP = \sum_{t=0}^{n} \frac{R_t - C_t}{(I + i)^t \, (I + i)^t} + \frac{X_n}{(I + i)^n \, (I + r)^n}$$

where
NVP = net present value of the investment;
R = annual expected gross revenues in future years;
C = annual expected costs in future years excluding interest and amortisation;
X = expected resale value of assets in year n when the investment is terminated;
i = the expected opportunity cost of capital in future years (in principle one may, of course, define discount rates that vary over time);
r = a discount factor to allow explicitly for risks arising from events not specifically associated with the project, such as political risks (in order to allow for risk more adequately, one should allow for the variance of these variables as well);
t = $0...n$, number of years over which returns are discounted, reflecting the planning horizon of the investor.

24. See Reuber, op. cit., p. 50.

25. Jüttner, "Förderung und Schutz deutscher Direktinvestitionen in Entwicklungsländern, Internationale Kooperation," *Aachener Studien zur internationalen technisch-wirtschaftlichen Zusammenarbeit*, 15, 1975, pp. 373-382; in this context, see also Delupis, *Finance and Protection of Investments in Developing Countries*, Epping, Essex, 1973, pp. 27 ff.

26. See Juhl, "Prospects for foreign Direct Investment in Developing Countries," in Giersch (ed.) *Reshaping the World Economic Order*, 1976, p. 173 (187).

27. See the review of indicators in Juhl, op. cit., p. 188.

28. Reuber, op. cit., pp. 101-134.

29. See, e.g., Hymer and Rowthorn, "Multinational Corporations and the international Oligopoly: The Non-American challenge," in Kindlerberger (ed.), *The International Corporations*, 1970. In this context, see also OECD, *Market Power and the Law*, 1970; and OECD, *Mergers and Competition Policy*, 1974; see finally Södersten, *International Economics*, 1971, p. 458.

30. See 1.3. in this chapter.

31. See U.N. ECOSOC Commission on Transnational Corporations, *Transnational Corporations in World Development*, op. cit., p. 56.

32. Drucker, "Multinationals and Developing Countries: Myths and Realities," *Foreign Affairs*, vol. 53, pp. 122 ff., (1974).

33. Bergsten, *The future of the International Economic Order: An Agenda for Research*, 1973, p. 18.

34. See Fels, "The Choice of Industry Mix in the Division of Labour between Developed and Developing Countries," *Weltwirtschaftliches Archiv.* vol. 108, pp. 71 ff. (1972); this paragraph draws heavily upon Juhl, op. cit., p. 174.

35. Cf. United Nations Industrial Development Organisation, *Lima Declaration and Plan of Action on Industrial Development and Cooperation* (26 March 1975), UNIDO ID/B/155/Addl. of 14 April 1975. The pertinent part of the Declaration (para. 28) reads: "... solemnly declare ... that in view of the low percentage share of the developing countries in total world industrial production ... their share should be increased to the maximum possible extent and as far as possible to at least 25 per cent of total world industrial production by the year 2000, while making every endeavour to ensure that the industrial growth so achieved is distributed among the developing countries as evenly as possible."

36. There remain some doubts concerning the effective share which is likely to be reached. According to various projections a share of about 14 per cent seems to be feasible; see Donges," Zur Industrialisierungsprojektion der UNIDO," *Bundesministerium für Wirtschaftliche Zusammenarbeit, Entwicklungspolitik, Materialien*, no. 52, Bonn, Dez. 1975, pp. 64 ff.

37. Wolter, " A sound Case for Relocation," *Intereconomics*, no. 12, pp. 366 ff. (1975).

38. The Conference Board, *Multinationals in Contention*, 1978, p. 43.

39. See the contribution of Wells in Cooper (ed.), *The Case for the Multinational Corporation*, New York, 1977.

40. Salomon, *Science et politique*, Paris, 1970.

Part two

National policies and international approaches

Chapter Four

MAIN TRENDS IN NATIONAL POLICIES

National governments and international governmental organisations are trying to create new arrangements, agreements, laws, and institutions to oversee and regulate relationships between TNEs and nation states with a view to achieving a more equitable allocation of the costs and benefits of TNE operations. While the nation states, i.e., the host and home countries, continue to be the most effective "regulators" of TNE activities and of the direct investment process in general, political entities at the intergovernmental level also seek, within the limits of their capacities, to survey and monitor the TNEs.

1. Different groups of countries and varying perceptions

The perspectives from which problems are viewed depend upon: (*i*) whether the respective governments dealing with the TNE are "home" country or "host" country governments;[1] and (*ii*) whether the host or home government has the perceptions and interests of a developing country or of a developed nation. In some cases, notably in Western Europe and North America, countries are both home and host to TNEs. Few TNEs are, on the other hand, headquartered in developing countries, although some of these countries (such as India, Brazil, Venezuela, Singapore and Hong Kong) have begun to develop their own TNEs. For the most part, however, TNEs are perceived as agents or instruments of the world's developed nations. Thus, there are four types of countries attempting to deal with the array of issues raised by TNEs (see Table 8.).

Table 8. *Developed and developing nations as "major" home and host countries*[2]

	Developed nations	Developing nations
"Host country"	Canada, Belgium, Denmark, France, Fed. Rep. of Germany, Ireland, Italy, Luxemboug, Netherlands, United Kingdom (EEC), Spain, Sweden, United States	Brazil Chile Indonesia Malaysia Nigeria Bolivia, Colombia, Ecuador, Peru, Venezuela (Andean Group)
"Home country"	United States United Kingdom Fed. Rep. of Germany France Switzerland Netherlands Sweden Japan Canada	India Brazil Singapore Hong Kong

Developed and developing nations alike — though to varying degrees — are concerned about the results of the TNE activities on trade and the balance-of-payments, employment and technology. Both groups of countries, especially if they find themselves in the position of host countries, may not only feel that foreign direct investment creates or reinforces economic, technological, and political dependencies but also has adverse effects in the social and cultural fields.

"Developed countries" and "developing countries" should not, of course, be considered as bloc entities, though the aggregate grouping of the actors in international economic conference diplomacy separates the OECD countries, the Eastern European socialist countries dominated by the USSR, and the developing countries (China either being included in this group of countries or considered as a fourth group). Though this grouping has the advantage of simplicity, it has a serious drawback: it tends to consider the various aggregates as homogeneous and does not allow for differentiation. While the homogeneity problem is posed in groups such as the OECD and the Eastern bloc, especially in a long-term perspective it is of much greater relevance for the developing countries, which are in very different social, economic, and political situations. The OPEC countries constitute a set of countries with similar problems, in spite of considerable dissimilarities. Another set is made up of countries like South Korea, Taiwan, Singapore, and Hong Kong, which already play an important part in international trade and investment issues. In some way they may be considered with countries which are committed to a process of rapid industrialisation such as Mexico Brazil, and Algeria. Another quite separate group is that of the very poor developing countries such as Chad, Bangladesh, etc. In between these and the more advanced developing countries is the long list of those countries which are normally called middle-income countries. There are, of course, factors common to all developing countries. Seen from Caracas, Lagos, or New Delhi, there are indeed some similarities in the vision of the existing political and economic international relations. Experience in multilateral conference diplomacy within the framework of the U.N. shows that historical resentment and certain common problems may create a feeling of solidarity among developing countries which frequently goes beyond immediate short-term interests.

Compared to developed countries, developing countries, when dealing with TNEs, often see themselves in a relatively uneasy situation: they are more vulnerable and their governments have fewer cards to play in the game. Their governmental institutions are often ill-equipped and insufficiently stable and lack the expertise and ability to oversee and monitor the activities of TNEs. Governments of developing nations are quite aware of the positive contributions that TNEs can make to industrial development but the perception of vulnerability resulting from the presence of foreign enterprises and the fear of dependence have a considerable influence on national policies towards TNEs. This has, in the case of some developing countries,[3] led to more elaborate regulation and growing control of the activities of TNEs.

The following survey of main trends in governmental policies pertaining to international direct investment and the activities of TNEs deals with the types of countries presented in Table 8; in addition, it also takes the Eastern European socialist countries into consideration. The pertinent developments taking place at the international level will then be considered in Chapter Five.

2. Host country policies

2.1. *A special group of industrialised "host countries": the socialist countries*

As far as the Eastern European socialist countries are concerned, direct investment as defined in this study is, as a rule, practically unknown, since it implies the existence of equity holdings, i.e., of control, which is difficult to reconcile with the system of ownership of the means of production prevailing in these countries.[4] That is not to say, however, that the activities of TNEs are of no real importance in planned economy countries. They are, in fact, tending to increase, but this is normally not accompanied by international transfer of ownership. Encouraged by public authorities in both East and West, interested enterprises — TNEs in particular, because of their financial and technological potential — have developed contractual arrangements with the socialist countries in Eastern Europe which go beyond the sale and purchase of goods and services and include a set of complementary or reciprocally matching operations in production, in the development and the transfer of technology, and in marketing. These arrangements and operations are usually referred to as "industrial cooperation".[5] The various institutional arrangements encompassed by this concept are basically regarded as an alternative to direct investment, since foreign

direct investment through the setting-up of wholly-owned subsidiaries is strictly controlled in socialist countries and, indeed,
as a rule, prohibited. Thus, given the absence of opportunities
for direct investment in the countries of Eastern Europe, as well
as the considerable payments constraints resulting from the lack
of convertible currency,[6] several forms of cooperation in the
industrial field have been developed. Generally, these industrial
cooperation agreements take one of five forms:[7] (*i*) coproduc-
tion and specialisation: i.e., both partners produce components
for a final product to be assembled by one partner; (*ii*) subcontracting: the socialist partner manufactures the product according to the Western partner's specifications and delivers the products to the Western partner; (*iii*) licensing: the Western enterprise licenses technology to the socialist partner, and payments
are made in the form of products resulting from the license;
(*iv*) turnkey plant: the Western partner is paid in the products
of the newly-created plant; (*v*) joint ventures: despite the
problems surrounding the concept of ownership, the socialist
country may, in the long run, prefer the joint venture, in part
because it gives the Western firm a substantial stake (in making
it partly profit-and-loss responsible) — in the successful use
and development of the technology it supplies. Thus, as Peder-
son observes,[8] this vested interest of the Western enterprise
assures the socialist partner that it will receive periodically
up-dated technology and that the Western firm will more fully
use its marketing outlets for the products of the cooperation.
At the same time, socialist countries benefit from Western technological and management experience.

The basis for these types of industrial cooperation, as well as
for economic West-East relations in general, has been laid down
by intergovernmental arrangements, agreements, and treaties
which provide the framework for industrial cooperation contracts between the respective partners.[9]

Notably in the field of joint ventures there might, in the long
run, exist considerable scope for mutually beneficial developments, as this form of cooperation seems to imply the greatest
advantages for both sides. From 1967 onwards several socialist
countries began to enact legislation[10] permitting participation

of foreign capital. The legislation of Rumania and Hungary permits the establishment of equity joint ventures in their respective territories. In addition to allowing joint ventures, Polish legislation provides for the establishment, in the case of small firms in the service sector, of wholly-owned foreign subsidiaries subject to certain requirements. In Bulgaria, combined cooperation contracts, based primarily on non-equity joint ventures, have been permitted. [11] Under all these legislations, joint ventures are predominantly channels for the transfer of technology. Finally, in Yugoslavia, the joint venture — because of Yugoslav social property concepts and worker self-management — would seem to be a quasi-equity one. [12]

In the short run, however, more simple forms of industrial cooperation, such as, sub-contracting, licenses, co-production and turn-key operations, will certainly prevail, because most Communist régimes are at present unwilling to accept even minor modifications of the basic concept of control of production and contacts with customers.

Although the various types of arrangements referred to above still account for only a modest share of total East-West trade (i.e., of the order of 4 to 5 per cent of trade in manufactures), industrial cooperation is generally acknowledged as playing an increasingly important role in the West-East transfer of technology. [13] Thus, the most frequent cooperation agreements are encountered in such technology-intensive sectors as engineering, chemicals, and transportation equipment, all of these being fields in which TNEs of the Western market economies are especially active.

It is finally important to note that, although small and medium-sized enterprises still play an important role in East-West trade, available data [14] seem to indicate that the majority of East-West industrial cooperation contracts have been entered into on the Western side by TNEs. There are several reasons for this phenomenon:

—TNEs may, in general, have special advantages in doing business with the East, because, due to their large size, they are able to be responsive to the socialist countries' policies. The Eastern partners also see the TNE as a more reliable partner in that the

TNE can more easily bail them out of a shortfall difficulty;
—when selling to an Eastern European country, or doing business in the framework of an industrial cooperation agreement, the TNE is usually able to comply with an Eastern request to supply products or component parts from a particular Western country with which the Eastern partner may have a bilateral trade surplus;
—a further advantage for the TNE again arises from the peculiar bilateralism constraint in East-West trade: TNEs, with their world-wide distribution network, can be particularly helpful when a Western partner is forced to accept Eastern goods in the framework of an industrial cooperation agreement;
—on the other hand, some TNEs may find production within an Eastern country attractive as a way of reducing costs, as labour costs in Communist countries are relatively low. Production in the East may also be seen as a means of off-setting the emerging countervailing power of multinational unionism, as in Eastern countries trade unions do in principle not have the power to strike.[15]

Thus, while the policies followed by Eastern European socialist countries generally do not permit direct investment activities within their territories, a number of cooperation schemes have been developed allowing for some degree of internationalization of industrial activity in the West-East context.

2.2. *Western market economies and developing countries*

2.2.1. *Basic considerations*

By their very nature TNEs have aims the common denominator of which is, under normal circumstances, optimum profit at the world level; this may be compared with "national" enterprises whose objective is to optimise profits at the national level. The objectives of government policies, on the other hand, are different from those of either national or transnational enterprises since their basic purpose is to improve the well-being of the country. TNEs are viewed with suspicion because their interests can never be precisely the same as the host country's, and because their loyalties may be divided. For the host country, it is essential that the effects of foreign direct investment on the

national economy do not conflict with its objectives in the field
of economic and social policy, including industrial, regional,
scientific, and employment policies.

However, just as foreign firms may not be bound by national
laws and regulations in their dealings with host countries, so
host countries have not always felt themselves bound by their
own laws in dealing with foreign firms. Foreign investors have
been treated at times in a discriminatory and arbitrary way.
Tension over foreign investment and business have existed as
long as business has been carried on in this form between nations; and expropriation, nationalisation and armed intervention
to protect property were not uncommon long before the era of
the TNE. [16]

Host countries fear that the activities of foreign firms may
result in a loss of independence and that important sectors, such
as technological development or even large parts of the national
economy, may be dominated by another country. An additional
concern in this context relates to the extraterritorial application
of laws and regulations. [17] Finally, typical host countries fear
that home country governments may seek to protect the interests of "their" TNEs without regard to the sovereignty of the
host country.

Tensions have also increased, observes Bergsten, [18] because
host countries are attempting to maximize their returns from
incoming foreign investments far more aggressively than in the
past. Four features, he says, differentiate the present situation
from the past: First, virtually all host countries, developed and
developing, are now adopting policies to control foreign investment closely, whereas only a few did so before. Second, these
policies are more explicit now and thus attract more notice in
the TNEs' home countries. Third, host country objectives become "much broader and deeper".

There is a general trend throughout the world such that governments accept responsibilities for an increasing number of
economic and social objectives (such as regional equity, better
income distribution, and the development of indigenous high
technology industries) in addition to the traditional macro-economic goals of full employment, price stability, and sustained

growth, and the basic governmental task, i.e. maintaining an ordered environment in which society can function. Thus, governments are seeking additional policy instruments to meet an additional number of policy targets.

The acceleration of international economic interpenetration implies, on the other hand, the possibility that external forces hinder — or assist — the successful use of both traditional and modern policy instruments. Thus, TNEs as the most significant engine of interpenetration, represent both a major threat to the success of internal policies and a major opportunity for help. This is the reason why certain host countries seek a greater influence in the business policies followed by foreign-controlled enterprises with the objective of increasing the likelihood that the subsidiary will respond positively to national policies of the host country, rather than to the global strategy of the corporate family. As a consequence, some host countries treat TNEs differently from local companies, though many do not. The main point in this development is not whether or not the policies are discriminatory; of significance is, as Bergsten notes, the clear intent to shift, as much as possible to the host country, the package of benefits brought by foreign-controlled enterprises, being subsidiaries of powerful TNEs.

Finally, as will be shown later on in more detail, fundamental changes in the world economy and the political and technological environment have put many host countries in a far stronger position than before, and host country policies concerning inward direct investment are now far more likely to succeed. Host countries now have, as Bergsten observes, a far wider array of options in pursuing their objectives. Not long ago, the TNE, in particular the TNE having its headquarters in the United States, was the only source of advanced technological know-how and superior management. Now, however, TNEs have lost much of their power, because the attributes which they once monopolised, and which could only be obtained in "package form", can be increasingly "unbundled"; the capital may be obtained from private markets, the technological know-how may be hired from a variety of sources, and the members of the techno-structure [19] have become the most mobile factor of production.

Management skills may be either hired from the original source country or have been developed as a result of the transfer of technology also in certain host countries.

The TNEs themselves with their tremendous capacity to adapt to changing environments within fairly broad limits [20] may, to a large extent, be able to abide by such new circumstances and policies. While still objecting seriously to policies which fundamentally impede their commercial activities, they may, e.g., become indifferent as to where to locate sizeable proportions of their production and how to finance it and may quite easily accommodate to host country requirements on a great number of the issues raised.

There are, on the other hand, limits to such governmental policies. If too many prospective investors refuse to invest under the conditions the host country is trying to impose, the latter would sense that it has pushed too hard and retreat on the least important of its concerns, until it finds the mix that will maximise its interests.

The cooperativeness of enterprises under foreign control is indeed not only promoted by the newly-powerful position and bargaining strength of the host countries, but it is also being further accelerated by certain host country policies designed to encourage inward direct investment.

The latter considerations round out the strategies of certain host countries: to maximise their returns they not only impose a set of restrictions upon foreign investors but also use interesting incentives, such as, e.g., grants, favourable tax treatment (as, for instance, accelerated depreciation), tax credits, exemption from indirect taxes or customs duties on capital goods, official credit facilities (loans on favourable terms, loan guarantees, interest subsidies). The greater the incentives, the further the enterprises are expected to move toward complying with the requests of host countries. Thus, to the extent that host countries possess the degree of bargaining power and leverage to effectively pursue their policy objectives — as in the case of most developed host countries and a certain number of relatively advanced developing countries playing an increasing role in international trade and investment issues — the traditional picture of the so-called dependencia syndrome painted by many authors would need considerable modification.

That the economic contributions of TNEs are widely recognised does not, however, mitigate tensions between them and the countries in which they operate. But the source of tension is never solely — and probably in many cases even not primarily — economic; tensions are created much more by the political and social impacts of foreign firms in the countries in which they operate. This consideration is important: if the source of tensions is really primarily political, the possible solutions to the problem must equally be political in character. We will come back to this reasoning in Part Three of the study.

It is useful to distinguish three specific phases in which national policies[21] have an impact on TNE activities: entry policies, operations policies, and exit policies.[22]

—Entry policies screen out unwanted investment or help — sometimes seconded by a judicious application of investment incentives and disincentives — to obtain a particular structure of investment. Such policies may close key sectors to foreign investment; require the membership of nationals on boards of directors or as key officers; require local equity participation and regulate foreign take-overs of local companies; and scrutinise the equity and debt financing of foreign investment;

—operations policies impose, for instance, special requirements on the choice of a legal form of business organisation; regulate the taxation of foreign firms; specify the eligibility of foreign forms for national incentive programs; regulate work and residence permits for expatriate officers and staff; and control the transfer of foreign licences to the national subsidiary and the payment of royalties and other fees to the parent company;

—exit policies finally centre for the most part on the requirements of restrictions affecting the repatriation of capital. These policies may also deal with disinvestment.

The net value of the contribution made by the TNE to the local economy, of course, depends on the concrete form the investments take and the industry or region that they affect.

It is quite understandable that in view of the complexity of the issues created by the existence and growth of international

direct investment and the activities of TNEs, government attitudes have many facets. What is more, these attitudes are con-
tinually changing and even a quasi-exhaustive list of existing
regulations would not give an accurate indication of the concrete attitudes taken by governments in their practical applications. In addition, some countries apply certain policies without
these policies being necessarily reflected in their legislation.

2.2.2. *Policies followed by Western market economies*

As has already been explained, by far the greatest part of TNE
activities take place in the developed world.

There are typical host countries such as Canada and Australia. Other countries, notably the United States, used to be
almost exclusively home countries. The host country experi-
ences of the United States and Japan have indeed been limited
for many years, a circumstance which came about for quite
different reasons: after 1945, the United States was the primary
source of capital; the inflow of American direct investment,
notably into the European manufacturing sectors, was, in fact,
fostered not only by U.S. technological advances and relatively
cheaper labour in Europe, but also by more efficient uses of
international and national capital markets and the pre-eminent
role of the dollar in the international monetary system. Under
these circumstances, non-American enterprises had few incentives for establishing operations in the United States' territory.
It is worthy to note that this trend has been, to some extent,
reserved by the recent inflow of European and Japanese investment into the USA; thus, the United States have in the meantime also acquired some characteristics of a host country — a
development that, in fact, has had a number of political and
legislative consequences. Japan, on the other hand, has, for
many years, carefully controlled the involvement of foreign
firms in her economy; the situation in Japan is now undergoing
rapid change.

Canada, the nations of Western Europe and Australia remain,
however, the most important host countries for TNEs within
the group of Western market economies, which (as has been
shown in Table 4 above) are still the areas where by far the

greatest share of direct investment operations take place.

An analysis of the pertinent laws and regulations, reports and other material dealing with inward direct investment[23] shows that the Western market economies belonging to the Organisation for Economic Cooperation and Development (OECD), which, notwithstanding their varying political and social outlooks, have a common adherence to the concept of values compatible with the aims of private enterprise in a market economy, in general, welcome foreign investment. The approach to foreign investment in the OECD area is, in conformity with the multilateral legal instruments on the "Liberalisation of Capital Movements"[24] and the application of the principle of "national treatment", based on an economic philosophy which favours the free international movement of capital and requires that enterprises under foreign control, once they are established and operating legally, are accorded treatment under the laws, regulations and administrative practices of the host countries, no less favourable than the treatment accorded in like situations to domestic enterprises.[25] Although special legislation concerning foreign investment and the conduct of TNEs is infrequent (the only countries among those studied which have enacted separate laws regulating foreign investments are Australia, Canada and Japan)[26] national laws regulating international transactions and various aspects of domestic economic activity usually include certain provisions which apply specifically to foreign investment of foreign enterprises. Under exchange control laws, for example, inward foreign investment in many instances requires prior authorisation, although this is frequently merely a formality. Thus all OECD countries, except the United States, the Federal Republic of Germany, and Switzerland, have some sort of a foreign exchange control apparatus. Some OECD countries use it in certain cases restrictively; in general it is used liberally. Originally such exchange controls were not introduced in these countries with the primary aim of preserving domestic ownership and control of the economy, but rather for balance-of-payments reasons. As balance-of-payments considerations have permitted, the respective countries have tended to rely progressively less on exchange control mechanisms in dealing with current payments. However, as an outgrowth of their earlier balance-of-payments problems, such countries now have the experience of a foreign exchange control apparatus capable of regulating capital imports.

While most OECD countries — notably these nations that are home to "their own" TNEs and, therefore, do not want to see them subject to restraints overseas — have refrained from imposing specific restrictions on foreign firms operating in their economies, many OECD countries are, nevertheless, concerned about the longer-term political and economic impacts of foreign investment. Thus, through one device or another, TNEs are, in many cases, singled out for special treatment in practice, if not in law. Entry requirements and the wide range of regulations to which they are subject once the investment is made have already been mentioned, as have the close watch over take-overs of certain firms and the sector in which foreign investment is excluded. Governments may, indeed, also limit markets by preferential procurement policies and the selective use of certain incentives.

In general, government policies toward inward direct investment appear to take the following main forms, none of which, however, excludes the others:
—Policies to encourage inward direct investment;
—Policies of nonintervention;
—Policies designed to strengthen domestic enterprises;
—Policies basically favourable to foreign direct investment, but nevertheless, (*a*) designed to supervise, i.e., in the concrete case, to restrict the setting-up of enterprises under foreign control, or, (*b*) to oversee and regulate them after their establishment. [27]

2.2.3. *Policies followed by developing countries*

Governments of developing countries deal with TNEs in a wide variety of ways to achieve varying objectives. Although their investment controls and regulations are diverse and complex, an attempt will be made to describe, in the following section, some of the most important policies and instruments. [28]

As was already noted, while only a few developed countries (notably Canada and Australia) have established special machinery and procedures allowing for a systematic evaluation of inward investment, most developing countries screen all proposed major investment prior to entry. Following such screening, the investment proposal is either rejected or the conditions of entry are defined. The effectiveness of this screening depends, of course, on the efficiency of the respective bureaucracies and the bargaining power of the developing country in question. [29] A country rich in resources which has already reached an advanced stage of development tends to be naturally more selective in regard to TNEs.

Screening criteria are not always precise and fixed standards for evaluating applications frequently do not exist. To the extent that such criteria exist, they normally include such items as job creation, the establishment of export-oriented industries, technology transfer, and the training of indigenous manpower.

While in virtually all host countries certain sectors are closed to foreign direct investment (e.g., national defence, the communications industries, such as the press, T.V. and radiobroadcasting), in a number of developing countries this has been extended to such sectors as power generation, public utilities, and services (e.g., Colombia, Ghana, India, Indonesia, Kenya, and Pakistan), wholesale and retail trade (e.g., Colombia, Ghana, India, Indonesia, Kenya, and Malaysia) and certain basic industries (e.g., petro-chemical in Mexico).

Foreign TNE operations are in some instances regulated through equity ownership rules. There seems to be a growing tendency for developing host governments to ask wholly-owned subsidiaries of TNEs to include local ownership participation or to seek joint ventures. Some developing countries are rather rigid in implementing these policies, others are relatively flexible and recognise that the degree of foreign ownership must depend to some extent on the nature of the project. Another way of increasing control over TNE operations in developing host countries is to ask indigenous participation in management. A major problem here is locating sufficiently qualified individuals.

The desire for national ownership or control has also led certain developing countries to restrict foreign capital to minority holdings in certain sectors. Several countries, such as Colombia, Iran, Iraq, Lybia, and Mexico have prescribed that domestic ownership should not generally be less than 51 per cent. The Nigerian government is now proposing to require in all sectors a minimum of 40 per cent of indigenous equity ownership. Through these regulations, Nigeria expects to achieve majority indigenous control over their economy in the near future.

A few host countries have developed formal policies, so-called fade-out policies, aimed at ensuring that the transition to full national ownership will actually take place. The rationale for such arrangements is that in those industrial sectors where effective and efficient local operations have become possible, foreign-owned or jointly-owned enterprises should be transferred to local ownership and management. While many observers welcome such fade-out arrangements, others are rather sceptical. In many cases the experience with fade-out arrangements does not, indeed, seem to be too encouraging so far and some countries have abandoned their fade-out legislation or it is in practice implemented in a rather flexible way. It might be mentioned in this context that, in recent years, the economic, political, and psychological disadvantages of extensive governmental involvement in society and in the economy have been perceived, and several countries in the developing world (Indonesia, Ghana and Peru, among others) have pulled back from too extensive centralization in the economic field.

In the field of natural resources, a number of developing countries have expropriated the assets of foreign enterprises, especially those in the petroleum and minerals sector. [30] Other developing countries have utilised 'renegotiation' of existing contractual arrangements as an alternative to expropriation. The latter concerns not only the mining and minerals sector; there are also cases in the manufacturing field where renegotiation has taken place.

Divestment of foreign holdings has been effected through legislation such as the "Foreign Exchange Regulation" in India, the "Enterprises Promotion Decree" in Nigeria, and similar legal enactments in some other countries, or through direct negotiations with foreign investors in cases where relatively few such enterprises are involved. Regarding these policies there exist, again, varying degrees of caution and flexibility. Thus, reduction in foreign holdings is often linked to stages of expansion of subsidiary operations until a pattern of ownership is reached which suits the purposes of the host country.

There is a growing effort on the side of many developing countries to intergrate TNE activities into national development plans and investment programs. Developing host countries recognize more and more that benefits gained from TNEs are necessary for expeditious development. Thus, many developing countries use incentive schemes to attract certain types of TNE investment or to encourage it in certain regions or sectors: Some developing nations specify sectors open to foreign direct investment rather than those in which it is precluded or restricted; such specifications usually coincide with incentive schemes. Incentives are seldom reserved to foreign investors exclusively, but TNEs are very often the main recipients.

A rather important number of developing host countries have a policy of limiting the flexibility of TNEs in intra-company financial transactions. Brazil and Colombia, for instance, generally prohibit royalty payments by the TNE subsidiary to the parent company. Algeria and Egypt, on the other hand, negotiate the extent to which intra-company payments can be made at the time when the TNE subsidiary is established in the respective host country.

Although many developing host countries belong to the Convention of the International Centre for Settlement of Investment Disputes, most developing countries handle disputes — notably those which arise out of the sets of controls described above — directly with the parties involved. Virtually all Latin American governments, and some in other geographic regions, require local procedures for dispute settlement. Establishment agreements between these countries and the TNE often contain the "Calvo"Clause [31] — a legal doctrine stipulating that TNE affiliates will not seek international adjudication or diplomatic protection. This clause becomes, in fact, a problem only when nationalisation or expropriation of foreign property is imminent.

3. Home country policies

Many developed nations, in particular Western industrialised countries, are, at the same time, major home and host countries for TNEs. Thus, the policies of these market economies are greatly influenced by their dual role as both home and host.

3.1 *Developing countries*

This dual role is in contrast with the virtually exclusive host role of most developing countries. Very few TNEs are headquartered in developing countries. Thus, though some of the developing countries have begun to develop their own TNEs, for the most part, TNEs are still perceived as agents or instruments of the world's developed nations.

3.2 *Eastern countries*

Regarding the Eastern European socialist countries, these are not perceived as typical home countries. This perception is not entirely correct: Eastern socialist countries have, in the West, established both equity and non-equity ventures as well as wholly-owned subsidiaries. In addition, since the beginning of the 1970s, joint ventures as well as wholly-owned subsidiaries have been set up by developed socialist countries in the developing countries. The number of such joint ventures is comparatively small, but the volume of Eastern direct investment both equity and non-equity in developing countries seems greater than Western investment in the East. [32]

3.3 *Developed countries*

As a result of their dual role developed market economies have exhibited a keen awareness of the repercussions of their policies towards TNEs. They are, as has been shown above, restrained from applying strict regulations and controls on TNEs head-quartered in other countries by the fear that "their" enterprises will be subject to similar controls abroad. In addition, most

OECD countries stick, in general, to liberal principles and are concerned about certain attempts to protect domestic markets and industries from foreign competition by controls on TNEs, as such policies might easily lead to new rounds of "beggar-thy-neighbour" policies which would further undermine the increasingly vulnerable international economic system. [33]

On the other hand, while traditionally most home countries encourage and — to some extent — protect TNE activities abroad, there has been a tendency in recent years for some home countries to be more cautious about such activities than in the past. Home country governments might be afraid that "their" TNEs will become hostages for their foreign policy, involving them in some political adventures abroad which might be detrimental to their national interest.

In an attempt to remove uncertainty in the investment climate, a number of developed market countries have concluded a series of investment agreements with developing countries. Since 1970 more than 50 agreements have been negotiated, notably with the Federal Republic of Germany, the Netherlands, Switzerland, the United Kingdom, and the United States of America. [34]

In a number of developed home countries, certain incentives are provided to encourage investment in developing countries. The available facilities can be grouped into the following categories: (*i*) investment guarantee schemes covering "political" or "noncommercial risks" (i.e., risks which are outside the investor's control and for which no commercial insurance is available); (*ii*) fiscal provisions for investment income from developing countries; (*iii*) information and promotion activities, particularly the financing of pre-investment and feasibility studies; (*iv*) cooperation between government aid agencies and private foreign investors; (*v*) government-sponsored investment corporations.[35] It should be stressed, however, that the possibilities for action on the part of the governments of traditional capital exporting countries, i.e., in particular the 13 countries which are members of the OECD Development Assistance Committee (DAC) and which have adopted the above policies, i.e., to stimulate the flow of private capital to developing countries, is rather limited. This for the following reason: while governments can relatively easily apply restrictive controls on overseas invest-ment, for example through exchange control, it is much more difficult to exert a positive influence on "their" TNEs, however elaborate the respective incentive measures may be, with direct effects on additional TNEs' investment activities.

On the other hand, there is increasing concern in the home countries about possible unfavourable effects of foreign direct investment and the activities of TNEs on employment ("export of jobs"), the balance-of-payments, and tax revenues through the outflow of capital and technology. To cite one example, in Sweden a Bill was passed in 1974 concerning outward foreign direct investment capital flows. While under a previous Act outward investment flows were evaluated primarily for their impact on the balance-of-payments, considerations have now been added relating to the impact on industrial and employ-ment policies. The Bill also deals with the external location of research and development facilities, noting that the outward migration of such facilities may have certain undesired effects on the national economy.[36]

4. Potential for conflict

Bearing the Swedish example in mind and being aware of the policies followed by host countries, in particular in the field of investment incentives, it is perhaps important at this stage of the analysis to realize that the main impact of the new global trend, which implies a shift in power and control over TNEs from home to host countries is on the traditional home coun-tries, i.e., the countries where the TNEs have their headquarters. The reasoning leading to this proposition is as follows:[37] if host countries are successful in their policies designed to achieve an increasing share of the benefits brought by TNEs, someone else might receive a decreasing share. As just outlined, this "loser" is not necessarily the TNEs themselves, which indeed may gain more from the incentives than they lose from the requirements. It is rather the home countries which, under certain circumstances, might be on the losing side of the new balance. As host country inducements may attract economic activity and jobs away from the home countries, the latter may increasingly find their national interests threatened by policies which discriminate in favour of enterprises under foreign control. It is, of course, conceivable that all parties, i.e. the host country, the enterprise, and the home country, will benefit from some of those investments. However, there is always the issue of how to divide the benefits even when all parties do gain. Many investments, notably in the manufacturing field, may be indifferent to location and, hence, as Bergsten observes, may be close to zero-sum games; in such cases, a decision that is one party's gain is another party's loss. Existing world demand for a product, for instance, may be relatively fixed in the short run, especially for the processed goods and high technology items which countries are avid to produce; thus, there may be a limit to total world exports. If the host country induced the subsidiary of a TNE, e.g., by favoured tax treatment, to export a certain share of its production in order to improve its balance-of-payments, the home countries' exports may decline. Similarly, the capital which the host country has received to construct a plant may not be automatically offset by other capital inflows into the home country. Similar shifts in benefits may occur with respect to jobs, technology, or other economic aspects of investment the outcome of which is altered by host country policies.

Thus, it might be recognized that host country policies which attempt by using all means available, to tilt the benefit of direct investment toward itself may, to the extent that this is successfully accomplished to an important degree, trigger off a potentially important new source of international conflict. To the extent that this is done through measures which produce results different from market-determined outcomes, there may indeed be a greater likelihood that this sort of clash will occur. The kinds of techniques used by governments both to attract and to constrain international direct investment have been described as the "largest non-tariff barriers of all". [38] Particularly from the point of view of the United States and other home countries, the clash of these national interests could become a central

problem of world economics and politics; international investment policy could replicate to an unfortunate degree the evolution of international trade policy in the inter-war period. It may
be recalled that at that time trade was the dominant source of
international economic exchange, and with the onset of the
depression, governments sought to increase their national shares
of the international benefits which resulted from trade. Other
countries did not accept such artificial diversion and this led to
an unfortunate chain reaction of retaliatory measures. There
were no international rules and institutions such as GATT to
deter and channel such conflict. The result was trade warfare,
and a deepening of the depression. Today, foreign direct investment and the activities of TNEs have, to some extent, replaced
traditional trade as the primary source of international economic exchange, and even without a new depression or a great inflation unsettling the international economic system, the struggle
for the international location of production will almost certainly continue to grow in both magnitude and impact in all countries concerned.

Indeed, international fora such as the OECD began some time
ago to deal with incentives, for instance tax subsidies, which
artificially induce enterprises to invest in certain countries. The
World Bank has recently started work in this field. These efforts
on an international level are of great importance, as some host
countries have begun to get involved in foreign direct investment activities of TNEs having their headquarters in their country. Thus, for several years the British government has made
foreign exchange available to U.K.-based firms only if these
could demonstrate that their foreign investments will benefit
the United Kingdom's balance-of-payments through exports and
profit remittances. The Swedish example has already been mentioned.

5. Résumé

In an attempt to make a résumé of what has been said in this
chapter, one might come to the following conclusions: the pro-

blems of international investment are increasingly complex and not conducive to generalisations. International investment has been growing in volume and economic and political importance; thus, inhabitants in one country are more and more affected — as consumers, employees, employers, investors, and suppliers of services— by decisions made in another country. The latter circumstance brought TNEs to the forefront of public attention as they have come to be seen to circumvent certain national or local policies. While a few TNEs are headquartered in developing countries and the Eastern socialist countries, for the most part, TNEs are perceived as instruments of the Western market economies. Host country governments, notably the leaders of developing countries, recognise the contribution made by TNEs to economic development. The bargaining power and leverage, in particular of the advanced developing countries in which the greatest part of TNE operations in developing countries take place, has increased; thus, many developing host countries have established screening procedures and a growing network of controls and regulations designed to tilt the benefits of foreign investment in the host countries' favour and to minimise the costs which can be associated with such investments. Although there exist certain restrictive tendencies in the Western market economies, the latter are in general still committed to basically liberal principles in the field of international investment.[39] This attitude is partly due to the fact that many developed nations are, at the same time, major home and host countries and are thus aware of the possible repercussions of their policies towards TNEs.

There is increasing concern in home countries about possible unfavourable effects of foreign direct investment, notably upon domestic employment, the balance-of-payments, and tax revenues. The host countries' policies designed to tilt the benefit of direct investment toward themselves might be considered by home countries as an artificial diversion of the benefits of international direct investment flows, and this could trigger off a new potential source of international conflict. Under these circumstances, the home countries may finally become the greatest challenge to the TNEs' flexibility.

While in this situation countries might, as in fact they normally do, seek particular solutions within the framework of bilateral agreements, there is clearly a need for intergovernmental cooperation on a multilateral level as a means for avoiding or at least easing the problems which foreign direct investment and the activities of TNEs may pose for the different countries and for the international economic system. Such intergovernmental cooperation would, at the same time, have to encourage the positive contributions of international direct investment; in particular, it would have to avoid a situation such that national governmental policies dealing with foreign direct investment are set up in isolation and without a clear understanding of the needs of other countries and of the requirements of the international economic situation. Otherwise, such policies might finally turn out to be counterproductive and detrimental for the respective countries as well as for the entire international economic system.

The following chapter examines pertinent intergovernmental arrangements and agreements.

Notes to chapter four

1. Home country = the country in which the TNE headquarters are located; host country = country in which TNE affiliate operations take place.

2. This is a modified version of Exhibit 1 presented in the research report from The Conference Board, *Multinationals in Contentions*, 1978, p. 5.

3. Vernon singles out Brazil, India, Iran, Mexico, and Nigeria; see Vernon, "Multinational Enterprises and National Governments: Exploration of an Uneasy Relationship", *Columbia Journal of World Business*, Summer 1976, p. 11.

4. It is for that reason that Eastern European countries have not been expressly mentioned in Table 8.

5. For more details, see United Nations Economic Commission for Europe, *Analytical Report on Industrial Cooperation among ECE countries*, U.N. Publication, Sales no. E.73.II.E.11; and *Industrial Cooperation and Transfer of Technology between ECE Member Countries: An analysis of recent developments*; TRADE/AC.3/R.9 (6 August, 1976).

6. This major aspect is covered in Lewis, "East-West Economic Relations", *OECD Observer* No. 92 (May 1978), p.3; see also Portes, "East European Debt in Long-term Perspective", 1977 (mimeo.).

7. See, e.g., Wilczynski, *Multinational Corporations and East-West Economic Cooperation*, Journal of World Trade Law, Journal, vol. 16 (May-June 1975), p. 271.

8. Pedersen, *Joint Ventures in the Soviet Union: A Legal and Economic Perspective*, Harvard International Law Journal, vol. 16 (Spring 1975), p. 390.

9. See United Nations Economic Commission for Europe, *Long-Term Agreements on Economic Cooperation and Trade*, TRADE/R.351 (18 October 1977).

10. More details on these institutional arrangements may be found in United Nations Economic Commission for Europe, *Legal Forms of Industrial Cooperation Practised by Countries Having Different Economic and Social Systems, With Particular Reference to Joint Ventures*, TRADE/AC.3/R.10 (15 October 1976).

11. See U.N. Commission on Transnational Corporations, *Transnational Corporations in World Development: A Re-examination*, E/C.10/38 (1978), p. 201.

12 See OECD, *Foreign Investment in Yugoslavia*,1974.

13. See U.N. Economic Commission for Europe, *Proceedings of the U.N. ECE Seminar on the Management of the Transfer of Technology within Industrial Cooperation*, ECE/SC.TECH./10 (16 February 1976).

14. See U.N. Commission for Transnational Corporations, *Transnational Corporations in World Development*, op. cit., p. 195; Levinson, *Vodka-Cola*, Paris 1977.

15. Wolf, "New Frontiers in East-West Trade", *European Business*, Autumn 1973, p. 29; the case of Poland shows new developments.

16. The conference Board, *Multinationals in Contention*, 1978, p. 23.

17. See Schreiber, *The Proper Reach of Territorial Jurisdiction*, Georgia Journal of International and Comparative Law, vol. 2 (1972), pp. 43-54.

18. Bergsten, "Coming Investment Wars", *Foreign Affairs*, vol. 53 (1974), pp. 135-152.

19. See Galbraith, *The New Industrial State*, 1967.

20. For an analysis of this flexibility see, e.g., Streeten, "The Multinational Enterprise and the Theory of Development Policy", *World Development*, vol. 1 (October 1973).

21. The following analysis is based on U.N. Centre on Transnational Corporations, *National Legislation and Regulations relating to Transnational Corporations* (Report of the Secretariat), E/C.10/8, Add.l. (January 12th, 1976); and Grewlich, *Direct Investment in the OECD countries*, 1978.

22. This conceptualisation was developed by Jean Boddewyn, "Western European Policies toward U.S. Investors", *The Bulletin* (New York University Graduate School of Business Administration, Institute of Finance), March 1974.

23. This analysis is based on a survey of the pertinent laws and regulations of OECD countries; as to Australia: Foreign Takeover Act 1972 (Amendment introduced 1975); Australian Industry Development Corporation Act 1970 (Amendments 1973, 1975). As to Austria: Foreign Exchange Regulation (*Devisengesetz*) 1946; Joint Stock Company Law (*Aktiengesetz*) 1965. As to Belgium-Luxembourg: Law to Promote Investment 1970. As to Canada: Foreign Investment Review Act 1974; Development Corporation Act 1971. As to France: Foreign Exchange Regulation, Decree No. 68-1021 of 24 November 1968; Foreign Investments, Decree No. 67-78 of 27 January 1967, as modified by Decrees No. 69-264 of 21 March 1969, and No. 71-143 of 22 February 1971. Federal Republic of Germany: Corporation Law (*Aktiengesetz*) 1965; Foreign Trade and Payments Law (*Aussenwirtschaftsgesetz*) 1961 and Regulation Implementing the Foreign Trade and Payments Law 1973. As to Italy: Law Governing Foreign Investment and Exchange Control, Law No. 43 of 7 February 1956; Regulations Pursuant to Law No. 43 Enacted as D.P.R. No. 758 of 6 July 1956. As to Japan: Foreign Investment Law, Law No. 163 of 10 May 1950 and amendments; Cabinet Order concerning the Acquisition of Properties and/or Rights by Foreign Nationals, Cabinet Order No. 51, 1949; Cabinet Decision concerning the Liberalisation of Foreign Investment in Japan, Cabinet Decision of 6 June 1967. As to the Netherlands: Exchange Control, Royal Decree of 1945, as amended in 1950, 1962. As to Switzerland: Agreement concerning Foreign Funds of 31 March 1964 (*Convention sur les Fonds étrangers, Recueil des lois fédérales,* 1964). As to the United Kingdom: Exchange Control Act 1947. United States: Foreign Investors Tax Act 1966; Foreign Investment Study Act 1974. See also OECD, *Interim Report of the Industry Committee on International Enterprises,* 1974; OECD, *Penetration of Multinational Enterprises in Manufacturing Industry in Member Countries,* 1977.

24. OECD, *Code of Liberalisation of Capital Movements,* Paris 1973; see also Grewlich, *Bedeutung und Funktionsweise des OECD-Kodex zur Liberalisierung des Kapitalverkehrs,* Recht der Internationalen Wirtschaft (1977), p. 252.

25. See OECD, "Declaration by the Governments of OECD Member Countries and Decisions of the OECD Council on Guidelines for Multinational Enterprises, National Treatment, International Investment Incentives and Disincentives and Consultation Procedures, OECD Council at Ministerial Level, 21-22 June 1976"; published as OECD, *International Investment and Multinational Enterprises,* 1976.

26. In Australia, the Companies (Foreign Takeovers) Act of 1973 is designed to control the foreign acquisition of ownership or control of Australian companies; new foreign investment is so far not covered by this act. The Canadian Foreign Investment Review Act of 1974 has a broader scope providing for the regulation of new foreign investment as well as takeovers. In Japan, the Foreign Investment Law, which dates back to 1950, has been repeatedly amended and foreign investment was primarily governed by a 1967 Cabinet Decision concerning the Liberalisation of Foreign Investment in Japan (there still exist industries, where restrictions have not been relaxed). In addition, a multiplicity of regulations are in force.

27. These different policies are explored in more detail in Grewlich, *Direct Investment in the OECD Countries*, 1978, pp. 50-63.

28. This survey is based on a review of the collections of host country laws and regulations contained in U.N. Centre on Transnational Corporations, *National Legislation and Regulations relating to Transnational Corporations*, op.cit.; and International Centre for Settlement of Investment Disputes, *Investment Laws of the World* (Dobbs Ferry, N.Y., Oceana), looseleaf; the section on "Host Country policies" contained in U.N. Commission on Transnational Corporations, *Transnational Corporations in World Development*, op.cit., pp. 19-24 as well as the pertinent part in Conference Board, *Multinationals in Contention*, op.cit., pp. 34-54 (and the case studies in chapter 5 of this research report from the Conference Board) have also been taken into consideration.

29. The U.N. Centre for Transnational Enterprises has launched a technical cooperation programme designed to strengthen the capacity of host countries, particularly developing countries, in their dealings with TNEs; see CTC Reporter, *Progress Report on the Technical Cooperation Programme*, vol. l, no. 2 (June 1977), p. 14.

30. For some views on nationalisation and the background to it, see Bostock and Harvey, *Economic Independence and Zambian Copper: A Case Study in Foreign Investment*, 1972; Böckstiegel, *Die allgemeinen Grundsätze des Völkerrechts über Eigentumsentziehung*, 1963; Girvan, *Corporate Imperialism: Conflict and Expropriation: Transnational Corporations and Economic Nationalism in the Third World*, 1976.

31. Carlos Calvo was an Argentine lawyer and diplomat whose treatises on international law, written in Spanish and French, have greatly influenced Latin-American legal thinking; cf. Calvo, *Le droit international théorique et pratique*, 5th ed., 1896.

32. Gutman and Arkwright, "Coopération industrielle tripartite Est-Ouest-Sud: Evaluation financière et analyse des modalités de paiement et de financement", *Politique Etrangère* vol. 41, no. 6 (1976), pp. 615-641.

33. Cf. the Communiqué issued at the end of the OECD Council Meeting at Ministerial level on 15 June 1978, *OECD Observer* No. 93 (July 1978), p. 4.

34. See International Chamber of Commerce, *Bilateral Treaties for International Investment* 1977; see also Chapter Three, section 2.2 above.

35. See OECD, *Investing in Developing Countries*, 1975.

36. Sammuelsson, *National Scientific and Technological Potential and the Activities of Multinational Corporations: The Case of Sweden*, Report to the OECD, 1975.

37. The following considerations draw heavily on Bergsten, *Coming Investment Wars*, op.cit.; cf. also Grewlich, op.cit., p. 67.

38. Safarian and Bell, "Issues Raised by National Control of the Multinational Corporation", *Columbia Journal of World Business* (Winter 1973), p. 16.

39. Cf. Declaration by OECD Governments, op.cit. (ref. note 25 in this chapter).

Chapter Five

INTERNATIONAL APPROACHES

Intergovernmental organisations and major non-governmental entities have, in recent years, initiated efforts at the international level designed to deal with issues pertaining to international investment and the activities of TNEs.

1. Categories and dimensions

International business organisations and a number of TNEs have established sets of guidelines emphasising the rights and responsibilities of TNEs and of home and host countries. The Guidelines of the International Chamber of Commerce[1] adopted in 1972, for instance, address themselves to these three parties. Another example is the guidelines adopted by the Pacific Basin Economic Council (PBEC).[2]

The international trade union movement has been active in the field since the late 1960s. According to the International Confederation of Free Trade Unions (ICFTU) Multinational Charter, adopted in 1975, the preferred solution would be a multilateral treaty and the establishment of a new specialised agency entrusted with the supervision of its implementation.[3] The European Trade Union Confederation (ETUC) has made demands to the member governments of the European Community (EC) and the European Free Trade Association (EFTA) that national and international controls be established to limit TNE activities; at the same time the ETUC is pressing for "economic democracy" and an EC-level system of collective bargaining.[4]

The International Labour Office (ILO) has been dealing with the question of TNEs since the early 1970s. Its Tripartite Declaration,[5] mentioned earlier, concentrates on employment training, working conditions, and industrial relations and is addressed to TNEs, employers' and workers' organisations, and governments.

The EC has dealt with some aspects of international investment. The OECD countries also saw the need for intergovernmental action concerning the issues pertaining to international investment and the activities of TNEs; in June 1976 these countries adopted a declaration, together with Guidelines for Multinational Enterprises, and three decisions on intergovernmental consultation procedures on the guidelines, national treatment and international investment incentives and disincentives.[6] Another international forum that has responded to TNE issues is the Andean Common Market (ANCOM).

In this context it might also be useful to refer to the International Centre for Settlement of Investment Disputes (ICSID), established under the auspices of the World Bank by the Convention on the Settlement of Disputes between States and Nationals of other States, which entered into force in 1966. By January 1978, 73 governments had signed the convention and 68 had ratified it, although most Latin American countries declined to participate. So far, however, only eight cases have been referred to the ICSID.[7]

In the General Assembly of the United Nations, several resolutions have been adopted which address themselves directly or indirectly to foreign private investment issues in earlier years. Later in the 1970s, TNEs found themselves the direct focus of the General Assembly's activities. At the same time particular directives were given in UNCTAD resolutions concerning the work on "restrictive business practices" and "the transfer of technology". The work of the U.N. ECOSOC Commission on Transnational Corporations, which came into operation in 1975 and is assisted by the Centre on Transnational Corporations, focuses in particular on the formulation of a code of conduct.[8]

Several ways may exist to group these international approaches. According to the level of authority, for instance one may distinguish between non-governmental (self-policing), intergovernmental and supra-national approaches. Another distinction might concern the objective and thus be drawn between those approaches that attempt to strengthen international cooperation and policy coordination in order to improve the international investment climate and those approaches seeking the "alteration of bargaining power".[9] While the traditional home countries of TNEs (OECD countries) do, in principle, follow the first approach, the latter is being pursued by developing countries and labour organisations which perceive themselves as disadvantaged in their relations with TNEs. Another important consideration finally concerns the legal nature, i.e. the question of whether the respective standards of behaviour, guidelines or rules are voluntary or legally binding, wholly or in part. Table 9 attempts to depict the different categories of approaches to international investment and the activities of TNEs.

Table 9. *International responses to the issues pertaining to international investment and the activities of TNEs*

Objective	Level of authority					
	Non-governmental		Inter-governmental		Supra-national	
	b	v	v	b	b	v
Policy coordination; improvement of international investment climate		ICC PBEC	OECD		EC	
"Alteration of bargaining power"		ICFTU ETUC	ILO	UN Code UNCTAD	ANCOM	

v = voluntary;   b = binding

The following sections discuss some of the most signicant efforts designed to deal with international investment and the activities of TNEs. Though this study deals primarily with intergovernmental organisations, some consideration will be given to certain approaches taken by international non-governmental organisations, notably the ICC and the international trade union movements.

2. International non-governmental approaches

2.1. *The business community*

Businesses have not been passive spectators to the development in national and intergovernmental policies relating to international investment. Like the trade unions, business organisations and business leaders have taken an active role in the process of national and intergovernmental policy-making. Firms, notably the TNEs, have been forced to develop new attitudes vis-à-vis their public identities and responsibilities. Enterprises can no longer think of the communities in which they do business in terms of environment, markets, and "outside world". Increasingly they have to understand this outside world and to cope with the interfaces of government, society, and business. [10] While this new openness of the business world certainly has many positive aspects, certain circles in national governments have, on the other hand, become concerned about the effects of a too far-reaching "openness" on their autonomy in the policy-making process.

There exist different opinions on the degree of openness and social responsibility to be observed by an enterprise. Basically there are two schools of thought. One holds that a businessman and his enterprise will best serve society by relentlessly pursuing efficiency and profit: the only responsibility of enterprises is to specialise in making profits, thus contributing to a prosperous economic system. [11] Such observers consider it quite enough, for the manager to worry about his economic function. It is the government's role, they usually believe, to check abuse, prescribe rules, and to remedy the social consequences of aggressive industrial activity. This belief is often accompanied by distrust of both the motives and capabilities of those businessmen who seem willing to enter the field of public interest or assume responsibility for the social consequences of economic activity. The other school of thought maintains that the corporation should expand its role to satisfy man's needs for education, recreation, self-esteem, social status, and other values and should itself be deeply involved in the solution of social problems.

While there are, of course, certain limits to the involvement of an enterprise in the issues of a social kind — one major limit being, for instance, the legitimate interest of the shareholders — a growing awareness seems to exist that economic, social, and political affairs are increasingly interrelated, that a large "private" corporation is, in fact, a "public institution" and that its management should be conducted under the guidance of implicit moral values constituting some sort of corporate conscience. Notably the TNEs the activities of which transcend national borders might have to assume a higher degree of responsibility in particular in the social field. TNEs are not exposed to the consistent countervailing power of one single national government, but to different policies of different countries. These policies vary in scope and content and may thus, to some extent, hamper the activities of TNEs; but they may possibly also allow for areas where industrial power is exercised without governmental control. To the extent that such uncontrolled areas and pockets exist (due to the lack of a "world government" with regulatory power or the absence of world-wide harmonisation of national policies) TNEs may indeed carry a special moral responsibility; i.e. a certain amount of self-regulation would compensate the lacuna of world-wide governmental policies. Ideally TNEs should thus strive to reconcile their economic responsibility with their respective responsibilities in the social and political fields. By such a *"dédoublement fonctionnel"*[12] the TNEs could help offset the lack of an efficient global intergovernmental system the task of which would be to check possible abuses of industrial power.

Enlightened businessmen have indeed already established sets of guidelines and standards of behaviour by which TNEs would regulate and police themselves; and "codes of good business conduct" have been adopted by a number of TNEs for their world-wide operations. [13] In some cases these measures may be protective or tactical; other instances reveal, however, a deep sence of moral responsibility and a great deal of foresight.

2.1.1. *Self-regulatory codes and guidelines*

The International Chamber of Commerce (ICC) has issued "Guidelines for International Investment", which attempt to provide standards for all parties concerned — investors as well as home and host countries. Such codes are not binding; they have no force in national law, nor have national governments assented to them in the form of an international declaration or convention. Some observers describe these codes as acts of enlightened self-interest, others denounce them as cynical and hypocritical "public relations" exercises. Experience shows that such codes are influential nonetheless. The codes have become benchmarks against which the behaviour of TNEs can be evaluated, and they serve as models for national policy and legislation and for refined guidelines and standards developed by international governmental organisations.

The ICC guidelines have been particularly influential. These cover investment policies, legal frameworks, labour policies, technology transfer, and commercial policies. Since these guidelines seek to be universal, they attempt to embrace the widest possible range of enterprises. Provisions are general and frequently only applicable "when appropriate". Since the adoption of these quidelines, the ICC has been very active in bringing them to the public's attention. Translations of the guidelines exist in many languages, and press conferences on these guidelines were organized by many national committees of the ICC.

In this context, it is appropriate to mention another effort undertaken by the ICC: the establishment of "recommendations to combat extortion and bribery in business transactions". [14] The recommendations are based on the idea that neither governments nor business alone can deal effectively with this problem and that, therefore, complementary and mutually-reinforcing action by both governments and the business community is necessary.

2.1.2. *Some ground rules for direct investors*

Personal discussions with a number of executives of major TNEs during the preparatory phase of this study have lead the author to the conclusion that many TNE executives are prepared to consider the following ground rules[15] for TNE activities in developing countries (these rules are already partly contained in existing codes of conduct):

—give local nationals a sense of participation by (*a*) training and employing nationals in higher management functions; (*b*) conducting some research locally wherever feasible. A good opening for the latter is, for instance, research into the particular technology that is most adaptable for use in the poorer countries themselves;

—avoid 100 per cent ownership for import-substitution-oriented ventures unless there are demonstrable and overriding arguments for it, such as the absence of competent partners and a lack of local capital. For export-oriented ventures, on the other hand, 100 per cent ownership may often be right;

—refrain from avoiding tax by manipulating charges for services and transactions on behalf of particular affiliates so as to disguise real earnings;

—agree to renegotiate agreements under certain circumstances where the conditions on which this contract was based have fundamentally changed, therefore, causing unforeseen distortions and thus rendering the contract unfair or oppressive to either of the parties;

—follow a policy of hiring out as much work as possible to local sub-contractors, service contractors, etc;

—refrain from buying out local companies in traditional fields dominated by local investors;

—avoid, as far as possible, special concessions not available to local businessmen.

2.2 *Trade Unions*

Unlike the ICC Guidelines, the International Confederation of Free Trade Unions (ICFTU) Charter is not intended for voluntary adoption but, rather, represents a framework for national and international legislation. Still, the Charter includes a list of "Social Obligations of TNEs" in the form of a code which could, as a first step, be voluntarily adopted by individual enterprises.

With a view to realising its demands for "economic democracy" (sometimes called "industrial democracy") the European Trade Union Confederation (ETUC) envisages more than a simple charter of TNE behaviour. The ETUC is, in particular, pressing for:

—labour representation on the boards of directors of the TNE's parent;

—consolidated, published accounts for each TNE group, including and identifying all affiliate activities. [16]

3. Intergovernmental approaches

Despite the attempts of governments to survey and monitor the activities of TNEs more effectively, many host and home country governments alike have found these measures inadequate. Intergovernmental organisations have, in the past, dealt in a rather fragmented way with the specific issues arising from TNE activities. Recently, however, certain organisations have undertaken to deal explicitly with TNE activities as a whole. Notably within the U.N. system, major efforts are underway to seek a world-wide response to TNEs, global activities.

The nature of the U.N. exercise is, of course, highly political as the respective efforts have become a reflection of the North-South debate in which the developing countries have sought to obtain an alteration of bargaining power in their favour. In addition, regional approaches undertaken by developing countries also exist. The Andean Common Market (ANCOM) originally comprising Bolivia, Chile, Colombia, Ecuador, and Peru, for instance, has been rather restrictive towards foreign direct investment, establishing stringent rules to coordinate the terms by which foreign TNEs are permitted to operate and thus attempting an alteration of bargaining power. [17] The intergovernmental agreements of ANCOM have, to some extent, become a model for many critics of TNEs world-wide. [18] In this sense the ANCOM policy towards TNEs marks an extreme position in the pattern of response at the international level.

The developed countries, on the other hand, have found regional or inter-regional international organisations useful in attempting to strengthen inter-governmental cooperation, to coordinate or harmonise national policies, and to deal with problems of overlapping jurisdiction in order to avoid potential trade and investment disequilibria and distortions and to encourage direct investment activities. The two organisations which have taken the most significant action in this field are the European Community (EC) and the OECD.

In the framework of the EC, two policy areas have particularly affected TNE operations: EC competition policy and EC industrial policy. To some extent these were conceived as positive responses to the penetration of the Common Market by U.S.-owned TNEs and were simultaneously used by the institutions of the EC as vehicles for furthering and enhancing integration of the Common Market.[19] The same considerations may apply to the European Company Statute Proposal. [20] The European Parliament has prepared a draft code of principles on TNEs and governments for forwarding to the Council and Commission of the EC (Lange/Gibbons Code). Naturally the EC countries, which all belong to the OECD, also played a key role in the process of the elaboration of the "OECD Declaration on International Investment and Multinational Enterprises".

3.1. *The OECD Declaration*

After several years of preparation and intensive negotiations, OECD member countries have agreed that governments should take measures to improve the investment climate and that TNEs should abide by certain standards of behaviour set forth in a series of guidelines. The agreement took the form of a declaration adopted by governments on the occasion of an OECD Council meeting at the ministerial level. [21] The negotiating process which finally led to this agreement had been initiated by a report on "Policy Perspectives for International Trade and Economic Relations," the so-called "Rey Report"[22] of 1972.

3.1.1. *The content*

It was not easy to reach such an agreement on the multilateral level, because, as has been pointed out above,[23] OECD countries have rather different positions. In view of this diversity and the complexity of the problems involved, OECD set itself a relatively limited task: to reach agreement on a multilateral political level in a short time on some basic principles governing investment relations among OECD countries. This is, of course, much less than a "GATT for International Investment"; it is, however, seen as a first step in an evolutionary process. But in fact it was also *the first step* since agreement on many of these matters had not previously been reached in any international forum. The emphasis of the agreement is on voluntary action and on a pragmatic rather than an overly legalistic approach to the problems, focusing on procedures which would bring possible questions to the OECD for consultation and further clarification. The consultation procedures are embodied in three decisions taken by the OECD Council at the same time and in combination with the declaration.

The main problem in the negotiating process was the achievement of a balance between the two essential elements of the declaration: on the one hand, the application of the principle of "national treatment", i.e., the principle that governments shall not discriminate against enterprises under foreign control in relation to domestic firms and, on the other hand, the recommendation to TNEs that they observe certain guidelines in their dealings with governments, groups, or individuals in the country where they operate. At the same time, a third point had to be included in the package, i.e., concerning the provisions on incentives and disincentives offered by governments to foreign direct investment.[24] It is rather obvious that in view of the different roles which foreign direct investment plays in the various OECD countries, in general, those countries having basically host country interests were proponents of the establishment of clear standards of behaviour for TNEs, whereas the countries having the home country perspective (such as the U.S.) were initially only seeking action on proposals dealing with national treatment and investment incentives and disincentives.

As to the structure of the OECD Declaration and the Decisions, [25] parts I, II and III of the Declaration and, particularly, the Annex to the Declaration containing the guidelines for Multinational Enterprises (which have been slightly revised in 1979 in the light of three years of experience) are to be considered as the substantive part of the investment package, whereas the Decisions are aimed at the operational aspects of the package through introducing the relevant procedures. In these Decisions, the OECD Council, taking note of the Declaration and therewith incorporating its substance into the preamble of these instruments, establishes the necessary procedures for intergovernmental consultations on the guidelines for TNEs, on national treatment, and on international investment incentives and disincentives. The consultation procedures on matters related to the Guidelines also provide, in particular, for appropriate mechanisms enabling the OECD Investment Committee to take into account the views of specific outside parties, i.e. the Business and Industry Advisory Committee to the OECD (BIAC) and the Trade Union Advisory Committee to the OECD (TUAC). [26]

The pragmatic approach of OECD to the subject is perhaps most evident in what is not included in the Guidelines: no attempt is made to define what a multinational corporation is since there exists substantial disagreement concerning the precise definition (differences generally focus on such questions as how much autonomy the affiliates may enjoy and what the percentage of domestic versus foreign holdings is). [27] It seems that agreement not to insist on the issue of the definition made it possible to reach an accord without protracted arguments among experts. The same holds true for much of the content of the eight items included in the Guidelines: general policies, disclosure of information, competition, financing, taxation; industrial relations, and science and technology.

In OECD's ministerial meeting of June 1976 there was con-

sensus that agreement on the Guidelines was an important political act. Some speakers indicated that they would like this
agreement to be the first step towards more binding rules. Others preferred the voluntary approach; the opinion was expressed
that the TNEs would, in fact, observe the Guidelines and that it
would be useful to have in OECD a forum where these matters
could be kept under review. Both BIAC and TUAC as well as
individual TNEs may be invited to participate in the respective
intergovernmental consultations, but in no case will OECD
reach conclusions on the conduct of individual TNEs. [28] It is
indeed these consultations on a periodic basis which may ensure
that the OECD Declaration is, in fact, more than a public relations exercise. As a result of the consultations the Declaration
and Decisions will be adapted to changing circumstances and
these "living instruments" thus may gradually receive a more
concrete meaning. Thus, the "law" will eventually become more
"intelligent" than the original "legislator".

While the OECD Guidelines are basically addressed to TNEs
and contain a set of standards of behaviour to be observed by
TNEs in their operations, the Guidelines also contain a few
governmental commitments. Of particular importance is the following sentence: "Member countries set forth the following
Guidelines for Multinational Enterprises with the understanding
that Member countries will fulfil their responsibilities to treat
enterprises equitably and in accordance with international law
and international agreements, as well as contractual obligations
to which they have subscribed." This sentence shows that
OECD countries are convinced that established principles of
international law do exist in this area, a view which has been
strongly contested by developing countries in the course of the
discussions on the "new international economic order", as reflected in the instruments adopted by the 6th Special Session of
the U.N. General Assembly. It might be recalled here that this
is, in fact, not the first time that OECD countries are dealing
with the issues pertaining to the protection of foreign property
on a multilateral level. In 1962 an OECD Committee established
a "Draft Convention on the Protection of Foreign Property". [29]
While this convention was never put into effect, the OECD

Council passed, however, on 12 October 1967, a Resolution associating itself with this draft Convention and authorising it for publication.

In accepting the principle of national treatment OECD countries recognise that it is fair and in conformity with the general interest that foreigners and enterprises under foreign control legally operating within the national territory of the respective countries should, as a matter of principle, be treated as favourably as their own nationals and domestic enterprises from the point of view of the rights necessary for the normal exercise of an economic activity. Formal recognition of this principle confirms rather than modifies the existing state of affairs, since, in practice, most Member countries already more or less comply with it. This is in line with OECD's concern with liberalising investment. It may be recalled that the "Code of Liberalisation of Capital Movements"[30] adopted in the early 1960s, encourages governments to allow the free entry and exit of foreign capital. The principle of national treatment attempts, on the other hand, to extend this even-handed treatment to the operations of foreign firms once they have entered the country and are legally operating.

The part of the Declaration dealing with international investment incentives and disincentives is not very explicit, and it may be open to question how and for what sort of reasons were OECD countries actually induced to seek solutions in a multilateral framework. What is probably behind this part of the Declaration are the issues which have been described in Chapter Four of this study:[31] some host countries may, under certain circumstances, be inclined to use all possible means to tilt the benefit of direct investment toward themselves; i.e., by using a judicious mix of investment incentives and disincentives they may obtain shifts in benefits from the home countries to themselves with respect to jobs, technology, or other economic aspects of investment. This may produce negative effects in the home country and give rise to concern, in particular to the extent that the host country measures lead to results which are different form the normal market-determined outcomes. Thus the real objective of this part of the Declaration is to provide a channel for consultation, review, or even disputes in order to avoid serious conflicts between home and host countries.

3.1.2. *Assessment*

In an attempt to make an assessment of the OECD Declaration one may come to the following conclusions:

—From a legal point of view the intergovernmental arrangements contained in the OECD Declaration on the Decisions are actually rather weak. They are not binding and contain no sanctions. On the other hand, it is clear that it is not the legal nature that is important; the real significance of these instruments, at least at the present stage, is to be seen in the fact that they allow for periodic consultations and survey sessions among OECD countries, and thus for a continuous multilateral assessment of the national and international economic and political situation, and on that basis for a constant effort to put the existing arrangements and agreements of foreign direct investment into practice. Such multilateral consultations and review sessions can also bring considerable political pressure on countries to follow, to the extent necessary for effective economic cooperation, liberal policies, i.e., to get rid of unjustifiable restrictions on foreign investment flows, to reduce the existing constraints concerning the operations of enterprises under foreign control and, in general, to avoid resorting to measures by which they could try to solve their own economic problems at the expense of other countries, with damaging consequences in the economic, social, and political fields.

—The Guidelines for Multinational Enterprises represent a new awareness by the industrialized countries that if they are to ensure the survival of liberalism, the "unacceptable face of capitalism" must be renounced. The Guidelines were worked out in consultation with trade unions (TUAC) and TNEs (BIAC) and thus represent a real effort toward collaboration among the principal parties involved. The Guidelines carry considerable weight of moral persuasion which will prompt governments, trade unions (see the Badger Case in Belgium), [32] and the public to condemn activities contrary to the recommendations. [33] TNEs have, on the other hand, seen the positive aspects of these

Guidelines, in particular those which afford the possibility of greater security for their investments; BIAC and a number of individual TNEs have officially taken a favourable attitude vis-à-vis the Guidelines. [34]

—Without going so far as to say that the OECD Declaration represents a model for a more universal code of conduct, [35] it must be recognized that the Guidelines make an attempt to define Western business doctrine in the field of international investment and, at the same time, to break new ground in a complex and controversial domain.

—The Guidelines, in particular, may act as a "bridge" [36] between the pertinent work of the OECD and the efforts underway in the United Nations and its specialised institutions (they have already served as a broad framework for the ILO Tripartite Declaration of Principles). On the other hand, the Guidelines and the other parts of the Declaration cannot be simply extended as they stand into other less economically developed parts of the world. Appropriate adaptations would be necessary. The development of the Declaration and, in particular, of the Guidelines, has helped the OECD countries to clarify their position and to agree upon a common platform. At the same time, however, most OECD nations do not want to appear to be creating a bloc-to-bloc approach regarding the efforts underway in the United Nations, notably in the ECOSOC Commission on Transnational Corporations.

3.2. *The United Nations*

The U.N. approach to international investment and the issues pertaining to the activities of TNEs is the most universal but, at the same time, runs into the most difficulties. To put it in simple words, what transpires in the bargaining process taking place in the U.N. framework is an apparent confrontation between those trying to preserve the status quo by improving it and those who want to change it — sometimes radically. Developing countries ask to participate fully in the existing international system to gain full and immediate access to the system and an equal right to all its benefits. Under these circumstances

TNEs can expect to remain, for some time to come, a major subject for discussion and intensive bargaining in the international arena. [37]

3.2.1. *History*

For a long time, U.N. efforts to deal with TNEs have been fragmented and have focused on specific issues. The recent creation of the Commission on Transnational Corporations (CTC) and the Centre on Transnational Corporations provides, however, for a central focus that enables the U.N. system to consider the transnational phenomenon in a comprehensive manner.

The Havana Charter, [38] which covered various issues of international economic relations and economic development, dealt, in Articles 12 and 46-54 with foreign direct investment and restrictive business practices. This Charter, signed in 1948 but never put into effect, recognized the basic value of foreign direct investment and made an attempt to strike a balance between the need to encourage prospective investors on the one hand and the legitimate interest of the host countries to control foreign direct investment to a reasonable extent. Thus, capital importing countries undertook to "provide reasonable security for existing and future investment" and to avoid "unreasonable and unjustifiable actions" against the interests of the investor. On the other hand, such countries had, to some extent, the right to interfere in foreign investment through screening, restrictions on the ownership of enterprises, and any other "reasonable requirements".

Right after it became operational, the U.N. ECOSOC made another initiative which had no follow-up. It requested its Sub-Commission on Development to commence a study with a view to making recommendations regarding the need for an international code on foreign direct investment, which would cover, inter alia, the protection of the interests of host countries as well as the protection of investors. [39]

In 1952, the U.N. General Assembly adopted a resolution proclaiming the principle of permanent sovereignty over natural resources, [40] which affects foreign direct investment in the resource industries; in 1953, ECOSOC considered a draft of a convention on restrictive business practices which would also have an effect on international direct investment; and in 1954, the General Assembly adopted a resolution concerning the encouragement of foreign private investment,[41] the aim of which was to facilitate direct investment through the avoidance of discrimination and the conclusion of agreements among states for the encouragement of private foreign enterprises.

There are a number of resolutions issued in the last ten years by the General Assembly of the U.N. which have touched upon issues relating to foreign direct investment. They deal with the principle of permanent sovereignty over national resources,[42] the International Development Strategy of the Second United Nations Development Decade and concern, in particular, issues pertaining to the "new economic order", such as, e.g., the resolutions of the U.N. Conference on Trade and Development (UNCTAD)[43] and the resolutions of the Sixth and Seventh Special Sessions of the U.N. General Assembly, as well as the resolution of 1974 on a Charter of the Economic Rights and Duties of States.[44] The latter resolution is of particular importance as it declares in Chapter II, Article 2, that every state is entitled "to nationalise, expropriate or transfer ownership of foreign property, in which case appropriate compensation should be paid by the State adopting such measures, taking into account its relevant laws and regulations ... where the question of compensation gives rise to a controversy, it shall be settled under the domestic law of the nationalising State ...". This resolution thus denies the existence of established principles of public international law governing the compensation for nationalisation of foreign property[45] and refers exclusively to the law of the nationalising state.[46]

By the late 1960s, interest within the U.N. system of international investment and TNEs had become a part of the broader issues of economic development and North-South relations. This circumstance clearly reflects the political phenomenon that the initiative in the U.N. General Assembly had passed from the founding members and the industrial nations to the developing countries.

Questions relating to the establishment of a new international economic system will be discussed in the following chapter; but before that, it is necessary to reach a fair level of understanding of the structure and depth of the U.N. response to TNEs. The following paragraphs, therefore, consider the pertinent efforts undertaken by a number of U.N. bodies, such as UNCTAD, UNIDO, ILO, UNESCO, and ECOSOC.

3.2.2. *UNCTAD, UNIDO, ILO and UNESCO*

UNCTAD's main task, as perceived by the developing countries, is to play a major role in the efforts undertaken by the developing countries to alter the bargaining power between the developed and developing countries. Thus UNCTAD is becoming the major forum for the discussion of the economic problems of the Third World. The Second, and particularly the Third United Nations Conference on Trade and Development initiated work on restrictive business practices and on the preparation of an international code of conduct on the transfer of technology.[47] The formulation of the latter has, in the meantime, reached the final stage. Multilaterally agreed-upon principles for the control of restrictive practices are also being negotiated. Both exercises are of major relevance to TNE operations. Their actual impact, of course, depends upon the interpretation of the political, economic, and legal nature of the respective instruments.

Another response to TNE activities is included in UNIDO's Lima Declaration.[48] This document contains the statement that the activities of TNEs should be subject to regulation and supervision in order to ensure that these activities are compatible with the development plans and policies of the host countries, taking into account relevant international codes of conduct and other instruments.

The ILO has been dealing with the question of TNEs since the early 1970s. On 16 November 1977, the Governing Body of the ILO approved the Tripartite Declaration of Principles on Multinational Enterprises and Social Policy.[49] Its character is voluntary. The Declaration of Principles concentrates on employment training, working conditions, and industrial relations; it is addressed to TNEs, employers' and workers' organisations, and governments. The ILO Governing Body has proposed that the Declaration should be appropriately incorporated into the future U.N. Code of Conduct, preferably as a separate code on employment and labour questions.

In the meantime, UNESCO has also discovered an interest in TNEs, "which serve as an element in the policy of exploitation of the developed powers, thus constituting one of the manifest obstacles to the establishment of a new international economic order"(!). UNESCO's Twentieth General Conference has, therefore, decided in November 1978 that this organisation should also contribute to the preparation of international instruments regulating and controlling the activities of TNEs. This is another example of the amazing proliferation of organisations, committees, and commissions dealing with issues pertaining to TNEs. One may wonder if this leads to solutions for the pertinent questions or if this proliferation of work dealing with TNEs does not add to the existing confusion and obscurity.

3.2.3. *ECOSOC*

ECOSOC is the central focus of the U.N. activities pertaining to TNEs and international investment. In 1972 by unanimous resolution, ECOSOC requested the U.N. Secretary-General to initiate a study on the role of TNEs in world development and to appoint a group of twenty "Eminent Persons", form both developed and developing countries and of various backgrounds, to examine the impact of TNEs on world development and international relations. The work of this group [50] led to the creation of a permanent intergovernmental body, the U.N. Commission on Transnational Corporations, organised as a subsidiary body of ECOSOC and entrusted with the task of dealing with a broad range of issues relating to TNEs. [51]

At the same time ECOSOC created a Centre on Transnational Corporations as an autonomous body in the U.N. Secretariat. The Centre assists the Commission in its work; it has in the meantime acquired considerable influence and competence. The task of the Commission and of the Centre on Transnational Enterprises is to formulate a code of conduct, to develop a comprehensive information system on the activities of TNEs, and to undertake particular research and studies on the economic and social effects of TNEs and to establish programmes of technical cooperation with requesting governments (developing countries).

The Commission acts as a forum within the U.N. system for the comprehensive consideration of issues pertaining to TNEs and promotes the exchange of views among governments, intergovernmental organisations, trade unions, business, consumer and other relevant groups. The Commission has established three intergovernmental Working Groups: one Group deals with the elaboration of a Code of Conduct; another Group has to report to the Commission on further steps to be taken in the area of accounting and reporting; the third deals with the problem of corrupt practices ("illicit payments").

Among all these tasks, the U.N. Commission on Transnational Corporations has given the highest priority to the formulation of a Code of Conduct. The Commission thus seems to recognise that one of the more important aspects of the evolution of a new international economic system is the establishment of a balanced framework containing rights and duties for governments and TNEs, which would allow the TNEs to make an optimum contribution to world welfare and particularly economic development.

The following chapter deals with the process leading to a new international economic system. On this basis consideration will be given to the elaboration of a world-wide framework for direct investment and transnational enterprises.

Notes to chapter five

1. International Chamber of Commerce (ICC) Guidelines for International Investment were adopted unanimously by the Council of the ICC at its 120th Session, 29 November 1972, 2nd ed., Paris 1974.

2. The Pacific Basin Economic Council (PBEC) was organised in 1966 as an informal organisation of senior business executives representing major TNEs in its five member countries (Australia, Canada, Japan, New Zealand, and the United States).

3. International Confederation of Trade Unions Charter on Multinational Enterprises (Mexico 1975).

4. See European Trade Union Confederation Executive Committee paper, *Demands of the European Trade Union Confederation for Company Law Regulations for Multinational Enterprises* (Konzerne), Brussels 1975; see also Roberts and Liebhaberg, "The European Trade Union Confederation: Influence of Regionalism, Détente and Multinationals," *British Journal of Industrial Relations*, vol. XIV (1976), pp. 261-273. In addition, see the Resolution of the London Congress of the ETUC on the Democratization of the Economy — Multinational Groups of Companies (22-24 April 1976).

5. See note 17 in Chapter Two.

6. See note 25 in Chapter Four.

7. International Centre for the Settlement of Investment Disputes, *11th Annual Report, 1976/77*, Washington 1977. The Convention sets out the structure of the conciliation process (Articles 28-35) and the structure of its arbitration process; International Centre for the Settlement of Investment Disputes, *Convention on the Settlement of Investment Disputes between States and Nationals of other States* Doc. ICSID/2, entered into force: 14 October 1966.

8. See U.N. Economic and Social Council Resolution 1908 (LVII) of 12 August 1974; Economic and Social Council Resolution 1913 (LVII) of 11 December 1974; and U.N. General Assembly Resolution 3514 (XXX) of 15 December 1975.

9. Cf. Koehan and Van Doorn, "The Multinational Firm and International Regulation," in Bergsten and Krause (eds.), *World Politics and International Economics*, Washington D.C., 1975, pp. 191-192.

10. See Johnson, *Government-Business Relations*, 1965; Andrews, *The Concept of Corporate Strategy*, 1971; Shonfield, *Modern Capitalism: the Changing Balance of Public and Private Power*, 1965; Jacoby, *Corporate Power and Social Responsibility*, 1973.

11. Friedman, *Capitalism and Freedom*, 1962, p. 133.

12. Scelle, *Précis de droit des gens*, vol. II, 1934, pp. 450-455.

13. For instance, Caterpillar, General Motors, Xerox, Ciba-Geigy, etc.

14. Adopted by the Council of the ICC, 29 November 1977; the recommendations have been published.

15. The discussions on this subject were based on the outline contained in Diebold Institute, *Business and Developing Countries*, 1973, p. 65.

16. See note 4 in this chapter.

17. A descriptive analysis of ANCOM is contained in Business International Corporation *Operating in Latin America's Integrating Markets: ANCOM/CACM/CARICOM/LAFTA*, New York, 1977.

18. Cf. ANCOM, *Common Régime of Treatment of Foreign Capital*

and Trademarks, Patents, Licences and Poyalties, Decision 24, Foreign Investment Code, December 1970, in 11 International Legal Materials 126 (1972).

19. See Allen, *Policing or Policy-Making? Competition Policy in the European Communities*; and Hodges, "Industrial Policy: A Directorate-General in Search of a Role," in Wallace and Webb (eds.), *Policy-Making in the European Communities*, London and New York, 1977; see also Ipsen, *Europäisches Gemeinschaftsrecht*, Tübingen 1972, p.S.50 ff. and p. 545 ff.

20. E.C. Commission, "Statute for European companies: Amended Proposal for a Regulation," *Bulletin of the European Communities*, Supplement 4/75.

21. See note 15 in Chapter Two. The Guidelines and the two other instruments contained in the OECD Declaration have been reviewed by OECD Ministers in 1979. Their contents were basically confirmed. Ministers did not change the Guidelines with the exception of one case not foreseen, when the Guidelines were drafted (the transfer of workers from a foreign affiliate for the purpose of unfairly influencing negotiations with employees), see *OECD Observer*, no. 99, p. 39 (1979).

22. OECD, *Policy Perspectives for International Trade and Economic Relations*, Paris 1972, pp. 63-66.

23. See Chapter Four, Sections 2.2 and 3.

24. See *OECD Observer*, no. 82 (1976), p. 12.

25. For a detailed analysis of the OECD Declaration and Decisions on International Investment and Multinational Enterprises: Grewlich, *Direct Investment in the OECD Countries*, 1978, pp. 88-104; see also Schwamm, *The OECD Guidelines for Multinational Enterprises*, Journal of World Trade Law, vol. 12 (1978), p. 342.

26. The reactions of these two advisory bodies (representing industry and the trade unions) to the declaration is contained in *OECD Observer*, no. 82 (1976), p. 16.

27. See Chapter Two dealing with the question of definitions.

28. Cf. *OECD Observer*, no. 82 (1976), p. 13.

29. OECD, *Draft Convention on the Protection of Foreign Property*, Paris, 1967.

30. For an analysis of the OECD Code of Liberalization of Capital Movements, see Grewlich, *Bedeutung und Funktionsweise des OECD-Kodex zur Liberalisierung des Kapitalverkehrs*, Recht der Internationalen Wirtschaft (1977), p. 252.

31. Chapter Four, Section 2.2.

32. See Vogelaar, "The Guidelines in Practice," *OECD Observer*, May 1977, pp. 7-8.

33. See Schwamm, op. cit., p. 350.

34. Declaration by BIAC, Europolitique, 30 June 1976, Bruxelles.

35. See Jacqueline Grapin, "Un échange de bons procédés," *Le*

Monde, 29 juin 1976, Paris: "C'est la première fois que la doctrine des affaires du monde occidental est clairement définie. Il peut s'agir là d'une charte de départ pour les relations avec les pays en voie de développement et d'un élément nouveau dans la négociation Nord-Sud pour la définition d'un nouvel ordre économique international."

36. See Schwamm, op. cit., p. 350.

37. See Conference Board, *Multinationals in Contention*, New York 1978, p. 230.

38. See U.N. Conference on Trade and Employment held at Havana, Cuba, from 21 November 1947 to 24 March 1948, *First Act and Related Documents*, U.N. Doc. 1948.

39. *Official Records of the Economic and Social Council*, U.N. Doc. E/255 (1947).

40. U.N. General Assembly Resolution 626 (VII); 1803 (XVII).

41. U.N. General Assembly Resolution 824 (IX).

42. In addition to the resolutions cited above in note 40, U.N. General Assembly Resolutions 2158 (XXI) and 2386 (XXIII) are of greatest importance in this respect.

43. See, for instance, Resolutions of UNCTAD Conference 25 (II), 33 (II), 73 (III), 39 (III) and Trade and Development Board 53 (XIII) and 74 (X).

44. U.N. General Assembly Resolution 3281 (XXIX).

45. For a legal analysis, see e.g., Schwarzenberger, *Foreign Investment and International Law*, 1969.

46. See in this context Chapter Three, section 2.2 dealing with political investment risks.

47. See United Nations Conference on Trade and Development, *Report of the Third Ad-Hoc Group of Experts on Restrictive Business Practices on its Fourth Session*, TD/B/C.2/AC.6/13 (1978); and *Report of the Intergovernmental Group of Experts on an International Code of Conduct on Transfer of Technology* TD/CODE/TOT/1 and TD/CODE/TOT/1/ Add.1.

48. See note 35 in Chapter Three.

49. See note 17 in Chapter Two.

50. U.N. Group of Eminent Persons, *The Impact of Multinational Corporations on Development and International Relations*, 5500/Rev. 1 — ST/ESA6. 1974.

51. U.N. General Assembly Resolution 3514 (XXX) of 15 December 1975.

Part three

Direct investment and transnational enterprises in a new international economic system

Chapter Six

TOWARD A NEW INTERNATIONAL
ECONOMIC SYSTEM

The North-South dialogue has reached a critical stage. The major issues in North-South relations are (*a*) the feasibility of overcoming the worst aspects of absolute poverty by the end of the century; and (*b*) the reshaping of the international economic system. These issues are interrelated: the demands for a new international economic order have their basic economic origins in — apart from a number of political circumstances resulting notably from historical developments (especially the colonial past) and the particular nature of the present relationships between developed and developing countries — the unfortunate gap between incomes of people in the industrial and developing countries. A new international economic system must be shaped in such a way that it provides a better chance to win the war against poverty.

1. The need for a new international economic system

The present international economic system is no longer working well for either the North or the South, though there are varying degrees of dissatisfaction. Unfortunately, there is as yet no political agreement on the fundamental principles on the basis on which a new international economic system could be established. There exists, however, a common understanding that, especially during the last decade, the world has changed and that there is a need for the evolution of common views on a new, realistic and imaginative concept for managing the world economic system, notably in order to achieve rapid development progress and a major reduction of poverty.[1] There is increasing vision reflected in the rhetoric of leadership, but the action still continues to lag. In the author's judgement it is unlikely that there will be sustained progress on either the basic human needs problems or the economic set of issues unless the two go together with a moral humanitarian impulse expressed in a mutually reinforcing way. Without that, it is unlikely that there will be any forward economic movement.[2] The truth is that development means development of people.

1.1. *The notion of a new international economic "system"*

What is at stake is a progressive, long, deep and unavoidable change in world relations. In view of this process, the concept of a new international economic "order" is not adequate because it conveys the idea that one conference could, in a limited amount of time, establish a new and permanent set of rules which would suddenly define a new kind of order (as it happened, for instance, in the case of the Congress of Vienna after the wars of Napoleon). On the contrary, many conferences, many deliberations and discussions, many confrontations will be necessary; it will be a process in which major crises will occur. This process will last, not for ten or twenty years, but at least for half a century.[3] It is for these reasons that the present study prefers the notion of "new international economic *system*" to the expression "new international economic *order*". The word "system" refers to systems analysis and thus to the idea of a world system[4] to be defined as the framework of all mechanisms, institutions, and political and socio-economic processes, both formal and informal, which link organisations and persons of different nations and regions.

The following sections contain some fundamental considerations pertaining to the need for a new international economic system, notably an assessment of the economic situation of different groups of developing countries and of existing international economic relations.

1.2. *The problems confronting the developing countries*

Despite the fact that the past quarter century has been a period of unprecedented change and progress in the developing world, some 800 million individuals continue to be trapped by conditions of life characterised by malnutrition, illiteracy, disease, hideous surroundings, high infant mortality, low life expectancy, i.e., conditions beneath any reasonable definition of human decency. These are, in short, the problems confronting the developing countries, in particular the low-income countries among them.[5]

1.2.1. *Domestic development priorities in low- and middle-income countries*

The obstacles that the developing countries face in accelerating progress are different in degree and kind, as are the tools at their command. The differences reflect the enormous diversity in their resource availabilities, economic structure, social and political traditions, entrepreneurial abilities and management skills, and in their relationships to the international economy.

1.2.1.1. Low-income countries

In the low-income countries (countries with annual income per person up to U.S. $250), poverty alleviation depends overwhelmingly on increasing agricultural productivity to raise the purchasing power of the small and marginal farmer and to create employment for the landless at higher wages. Strengthening the rural infrastructure to support these development efforts will be highly demanding of investment. To achieve the necessary levels of investment an increase in domestic savings will be required and, in particular, large inflows of concessional capital, i.e., official development aid provided on favourable terms by the developed countries. The TNEs' possibilities to contribute to the advancement of the low-income countries via their normal commercial activities seem to be limited at the present stage.

1.2.1.2. Middle-income countries

The middle-income developing countries are a heterogeneous group in their economic structure, development experience, and level of income per person. In general, their economic growth depends more closely than that of the low-income countries on international trade and capital markets. Progress in alleviating poverty in these countries is less hampered by the shortage of resources than in low-income countries but will nonetheless require strenuous efforts. For the middle-income developing countries, the main strategic choices relate to how industrial and trade policy should respond to changes in the international environment, and, of course, also to the fundamental question of the extent to which these countries might attempt to influence and change the structure of the international environment. The latter relates to the issues pertaining to the alteration of bargaining power. In particular, uncertainty about international trade and capital movements in the next years represent major problems for the middle-income countries. In most of them, efforts to sustain the growth of export earnings will have to be supplemented by measures to achieve a more broadly based expansion of domestic demand. The latter will also require, inter alia, an acceleration of agricultural development, requiring more investment in the physical infrastructure supporting agriculture. Measures to preserve the growth of foreign exchange earnings, on the other hand, include raising export incentives, increasing the domestic value added in manufactured goods exports, and — this consideration applies, in particular, to the more advanced developing countries — exporting a more diverse range of manufactured goods. In this context, TNEs may, to the extent that their investments comply with the respective development strategy, have a rather positive role to play; though, due to the well-known uncertainties, private risk capital which has been a major source of finance in developing countries in the past is now less readily available. The concerned governments might, therefore, consider whether a general improvement of the investment climate could augment the inflow of private capital and induce, in particular, the TNEs to undertake the sort of investments which are beneficial for both the enterprises and the host countries.

1.2.2. *International policy issues and implications for developing countries.*

Progress in the developing countries does not depend solely on domestic efforts. The latter must be reinforced by international action in a number of areas.

1.2.2.1. Trade

The most important of these areas is international trade. The international community faces a long period of shifting comparative advantage (though the increasing use of microprocessors might reverse existing trends in certain fields), and it is essential that countries be ready to accept and facilitate the changes in the industrial structure that this will involve.

Unfortunately, it is likely that the scope for the growth of exports as a whole from the developing to industrialised countries will be much more limited for the next decade than it was in the last two. The successful termination of the negotiations concerning the GATT-Tokyo round and the Lomé II agreement does not change the truth of this statement very much. The main reasons for this are the existing trade restrictions for sensitive sectors and the faltering pace of economic recovery in the industrialised countries. But precisely in considering how to accelerate growth in industrialised countries, the importance of links with developing countries should be recognized.[6] Twenty-five years ago, these links were imperceptible; today, they are significant.

The developing countries, too, face problems in adjusting to changing international trade patterns. The more advanced among them would have to establish programmes to diversify the product composition and markets of their manufactured exports. Promotion of trade among developing countries will require important changes in industrial incentive structures, reduction of those trade barriers which are not justified any more by the existence of "temporary" difficulties or the need to protect "infant industries", and the strengthening of the institutional infrastructure in international transport, communications, and finance.

As international specialisation increases, truly active and responsible participation by developing countries in international trade discussions will become more and more important in order to abolish the existing protectionist measures — to the extent that this is economically possible and equitable. Most partners in international trade would benefit from an equitable (i.e., not necessarily reciprocal) reduction of existing barriers and impediments.

For those developing countries that still depend heavily upon exports of a few primary commodities, a "common fund" scheme designed to reduce to some extent the fluctuation of prices and to compensate for temporary declines in import earnings (as does, notably, the Lomé system), is of great importance.

1.2.2.2. Investment

Even with the steady expansion of earnings from trade, resources available to the developing countries must be supplemented by an adequate inflow of appropriate technology and external capital. In the latter area, too, there are uncertainties. They relate to the chances of reducing the non-oil developing countries' balance-of-payments deficit which amounted, in 1978, to about $35 billion; to the rate of growth of private lending, the expansion of the lending capacity of multilateral financing institutions, the concrete solution of the debt problem, the availability of official development assistance (ODA), and notably also the amount of private risk capital, i.e., the future flow of direct investment to developing countries. As regards the attraction of foreign risk capital, in a number of cases the position of developing countries might improve if they would be prepared to complete existing incentive schemes[7] with solid insurance and guarantee provisions as a domestic measure and to adhere to direct investment standards to be observed by both governments and TNEs. Apart from this, it is, of course, recognized that the prospect of attracting further investment engagement and capital from abroad are very closely connected to the countries' ability to maintain political stability.

1.2.2.3. The fundamental issue

The major objectives of development should be to accelerate

economic growth and to reduce poverty. Unless economic growth in the developing countries can be substantially accelerated through adjustments in the global pattern of trade to reflect shifts in comparative advantage and an increased inflow of capital, including, in particular, private risk capital provided by direct investors and in particular TNEs, the presently inevitable increases in population will mean that the numbers of the absolute poor will remain unacceptably high.

The fundamental question is whether these objectives can be reached within the framework of the existing international economic system: i.e., is the world faced with a situation where continuous and actively pursued adjustment policies as a result of the recognition of the phenomenon of "interdependence" may solve most of the existing problems; or, is the only viable way of reshaping the international economic system the fast attainment of a policy of "structural change" by hammering out a "new international economic order"?

The international system of economic and trade relations which was devised thirty years ago no longer seems to be completely adequate for today's needs of the world community as a whole. The charge against that order in the past was that it worked well for the affluent and worked against the poor. Though major crises have been avoided, it cannot even be said now that the system works really well for the affluent. This is an additional incentive for evolving a new economic system.

1.3. *Problems of developed countries and the present state of the world economy*

International economic relations have reached a crossroads where a new orientation, which takes the past and present realities of the world economy fully into account, is required. What are these realities?

1.3.1. *History: the "old economic order"*

The "world economic conferences", which took place in the period between 1944-1948, opened the way to an increasing number of multilateral treaties to replace the "jungle law" and the bilateralism of the 1930s in international economic affairs.

A number of international economic organizations were established; these organisations aim notably at the following objectives: (*i*) economic cooperation, especially in the field of international trade, monetary affairs and development aid (International Monetary Fund 1944, World Bank 1944, General Agreement on Tariffs and Trade (GATT) 1947; (*ii*) special sectional regulations for commodity trade (cf. the international tin, coffee, grains, sugar, and olive oil agreements), for the law of the sea (cf. the fourth Geneva-Law of the Sea Conventions of 1958), for copyright law (cf. the Berne Convention of 1952), or for the settlement of investment disputes (cf. the World Bank Convention of 1965); (*iii*) greater regional economic cooperation in Europe, Africa, Latin America, and Asia (cf. the Regional Commissions of the U.N.). All these agreements, however, cover the field of international economic relations only partly; they do not form a comprehensive network, and they are too incomplete "to permit of their classification as a legal world order in economic affairs".[8] There is, for instance, no world-wide agreement on foreign direct investment and restrictive business practices, as the respective Articles of the Havana Charter[9] were never put into effect.

The present framework for international economic relations, agreed upon, in principle, at the Conferences of Bretton Woods (1944), Geneva (1947), and Havana (1948) and legally embodied in the IMF and GATT agreements, was shaped by U.S. economic theoretical thinking of the 1940s and by the political demands of the U.S., which, practically speaking, were similar to those which characterized the role played by Britain during its period of greatness. This "world economic order" was based on two fundamental principles: in monetary terms, the principle of fixed parities and the dollar standard (although the dollar was convertible into gold at the request of the central banks); in commercial terms the principle of nondiscrimination and free trade. This economic *pax americana* lasted until 15 August 1971, when President Nixon suspended the convertibility of the dollar.

It should be recalled that the U.S. came out of World War II as the unchallenged dominant economic power. This situation of political predominance of the U.S. meant, in fact, that the U.S. exercised what some called "structural power",[10] which was de facto legitimised by the consent of Western allies. The U.S. had the power to determine and enforce new rules for the system of international trade and financial relations, which materialised in such institutions as the IMF and the GATT, where, in practice, the role of the U.S. was pre-eminent; a contrario example of this pre-eminence is the non-ratification by the U.S. of the Havana Charter containing, inter alia, rules on international direct investment, because under this scheme the U.S. would not have enjoyed a *primus inter pares* status. The legitimacy of the U.S. structural power was reinforced by the fact that: (*i*) Western industrialised countries agreed, in principle, with the fundamental rules promoted by the U.S. (non-discrimination, reciprocity, decreasing barriers, etc.); (*ii*) the U.S. voluntarily abstained — certainly not always, but nevertheless in many instances — from promoting its own interests exclusively; in fact, the rules were, on the whole, mutually beneficial and, in some instances, self-denying for the U.S. itself. The ensuing liberalisation of trade and investment, the stabilisation of exchange rate parities after 1949, and the role of the dollar both as a reserve and a settlement currency, helped the rapid recovery of war-stricken countries and led to a period of growth of internal economies of Western countries as well as international trade at rates never experienced before: thus, world exports grew from $57.5 billion in 1950 to $566.7 billion in 1973.

1.3.2. *The deficiencies of the "old economic order"*

This mutually-beneficial setting of economic relations implemented by the U.S. as a dominant power (the "U.S.-TNEs" were the symbol of this dominance) contained, however, the seeds of its own disruption. Changes in the world economy increasingly brought to light the lacunae and deficiencies of the international economic system: the non-ratification of the Havana Charter, notably the non-application of its rules on restrictive business practices and international direct investment, as well as intergovernmental commodity agreements, meant that certain premises for the functioning of an international free enterprise market economy were not accepted from the very start.

The non-discrimination and liberalisation principles of the GATT [11] were increasingly eroded or limited in practice, for instance, by the following factors: the growing number of customs unions and free trade areas; the gradual abolishment of reciprocity obligations; the increasing use of so-called non-tariff barriers (NTBs); the rise to over 30 per cent of the share of TNEs in world exports, which means that international trade is, to a considerable extent, a matter of internal enterprise strategy; the fact that most countries are still following predominantly national economic policies, in spite of the fact that, due to the increasing economic interdependence, many issues which have been formerly religiously reserved for national control, such as interest rates, monetary supply, government budget policy, and unemployment assistance, now become accepted agenda items for summit and other international meetings. It is indeed quite astonishing that, so far, it has been possible to avoid major trade wars and protectionist chain reactions.

The abolition of the gold convertibility of the U.S. dollar on 15 August 1971, and the subsequent floating of exchange rates led to the world-wide non-observance and derogation of the parity and exchange rules of the IMF Agreement. One of the main reasons for this economic crisis was the refusal of both surplus and deficit nations (in particular the U.S. as the key currency nation) to endanger their national growth and full employment goals by a restrictive balance-of-payments policy; to reduce the rates of inflation by international coordination of domestic economic policies; and, thus, to remove foreign economic disequilibria by means of domestic adjustment processes. The 1976 amendment of the IMF Agreement legalised the system of floating currencies. Although the need for rules and guidelines for floating and balance-of-payments adjustments was emphasised, no truly effective agreement on these matters has been possible so far.

Following the monetary crises, there began in 1973, almost simultaneously in all industrial nations, the worst economic crisis since 1945, with high inflation rates, low or negative growth rates, balance-of-payments disequilibria, and extremely high unemployment figures. The sudden and important increase in in oil prices at the end of 1973 reinforced the already rather strong inflationary mechanism and compelled most governments of the developed economies to act to limit their trade deficits. Moreover, the growing interdependence of the developed economies which has accompanied their rapid growth had the effect of synchronizing national economic cycles which amplified the importance of the recession, resulting in a drop of investment and output, followed by an increase in unemployment — while the infaltionary process was not stopped.

Thus, the international economic system still is burdened by the extraordinary convergence of two destabilising economic forces: first, an acceleration of already-existent cost-push inflationary pressures related to productivity stagnation and also, inter alia, the growing "oligopolistic" ability of large enterprises and notably also unions to promote administered prices and wages; second, a sudden international income transfer of unprecedented proportions to oil-producing countries. The result is the prevailing domestic agony of simultaneous slow growth and high inflation and the external strains of balance-of-payments deficits which characterize the international economy.

Finally, in the present period, which is characterised by its potential for disorder, it turns out that the absence of an international agreement, even in principle, on a universal system of rules and procedures for international investment is a major disadvantage. For too long a time, investment policy was, in fact, an orphan within the international economic system. As a result, investment policy is subject to various special arrangements on a less-than-universal basis. In many instances, there are provisions for conditions of establishment in bilateral treaties of commerce and navigation. The OECD has, as noted earlier, an investment code that presents general principles of free capital movements among members, which has been completed in recent years by the principle of national treatment, an instrument dealing with investment incentives and disincentives and guidelines for multinational enterprises. The EEC Treaty asks, in Ar-

ticles 67 and 71, the members of the EC to abolish restrictions
on resident capital movements within the Community "to the
extent necessary for the proper functioning of the Common
Market". These instruments might play a useful role within the
respective regions. Due to their lack of universality they are,
however, not able to serve adequately the international economic system.

Under present international economic conditions there is an
increasing danger of conflict in the field of international investment, notably as host countries might try to achieve an increasing share of the benefits brought by TNE operations; "investment wars" might be the result of distortions of direct investment flows. This delicate situation was explained above in
Chapter Four. Thus, the process of reshaping the international
economic system should not only concern the areas of trade,
commodities, energy, and monetary affairs, but should also
clearly comprise international investment and the activities of
TNEs.

2.   The process leading to a new international economic system

The economic problems of the developed countries as a whole,
as well as the existing potential for conflicts among these countries, could probably have been important enough forces of
adjustment and change to lead to a new pattern of international
relationships. But the pressure for a "new international economic order" explicitly came from the less developed countries or
rather from the most radical fraction who succeeded in uniting
around it an ever-growing number of Third World countries.

2.1   *The demand for a "new international economic order": its
political, legal, and ideological aspects; the skeptics' view;
"inner limits"*

The main demands of the U.N. Declaration on the Establishment of a New International Economic Order, the Programme
of Action and the Charter of Economic Rights and Duties of

States, [12] are not new and are already contained in earlier U.N. and UNCTAD Resolutions. Taken together, they do not constitute a coherent system for a "new international economic order", but rather a list of sometimes inconsistent demands relating to development and to North-South relations without a consistent overall concept; (there are, just to mention one lacuna, no rules concerning East-West trade). The surprise of the Western industrialised countries in 1974 stemmed from the sudden coalescence of virtually the entire developing world around a common position requiring a change in the structure and mechanisms of international economic relationships and going far beyond the hitherto existing development policies and institutions. The Western market economies had to realise that the Southern coalition in the U.N. began to shift its tactics away from demands for concessions on tariffs and for more aid to demands for changes in present economic institutions which were accused of perpetuating existing inequalities in the world.

Whereas the Declaration and the Charter are essentially limited to vaguely formulated principles, the Programme of Action contains an abundance of operative demands, also for those branches of the international economy which were excluded from the Declaration and the Charter (e.g., international monetary relations). The respective demands are addressed predominantly to OECD countries and only in a few cases to Communist states as well.

2.1.1. *The major propositions*

The Declaration states that the new international economic order should be founded "on equity, sovereign equality, interdependence, common interest and cooperation among all States." "Equity" is the fundamental principle which should resolve the contradictions between the simultaneous demands for economic independence, for equality and mutual benefit and, on the other hand, for organized solidarity, systematic preferential treatment for developing countries and the renouncing of reciprocity.

The most important demands in the Declaration and Action Programme are as follows:

—adoption of an "integrated" approach to price supports for an entire group of developing country commodity exports;

—the "indexation" of developing country export prices to tie them to rising prices of developed countries' manufactured exports;

—the securing of official development assistance to reach the target of 0.7 per cent of GNP of the developed countries;

—the linkage of development aid with the creation of Special Drawing Rights (SDRs);

—the negotiated "redeployment" of some developed countries' industries to developing countries;

—the lowering of tariffs on the exports of manufacturers from developing countries;

—the development of an international food programme;

—the establishment of mechanisms for the transfer of technology to developing countries separate from direct capital investment.

The Charter of Economic Rights and Duties of States adds several controversial propositions, which will be dealt with later on.

Reference also has to be made in this context to other instruments postulating a new international economic order such as the concluding resolution of the Paris Conference on International Economic Cooperation in 1977 and to the Lima Declaration and Plan of Action on Industrial Development and Cooperation of 26 March 1975, adopted by the United Nations Development Organisation (UNIDO). Paragraph 28 of the Lima Declaration postulates that the share of developing countries in world industrial production "should be increased to a maximum possible extent and as far as possible to at least 25 per cent of total world industrial production by the year 2000, while making every endeavour that the industrial growth so achieved is distributed among the developing countries as evenly as possible." The chances of success for this "25 per cent target" have already been discussed in Chapter Three above.

2.1.2. *Particular demands concerning TNEs and direct investment*

The Programme of Action contains, in Section V, reference to dealing with the "regulation and control over the activities of transnational corporations," the demand to adopt and implement an international code of conduct for TNEs. This section notably makes mention of five items to be included in such a code:

—prevent interference in the internal affairs of the countries where TNEs operate;

—regulate TNE activities in host countries so as to eliminate restrictive business practices and ensure conformity of these activities with national development plans; facilitate in this context, the review and revision of previously-concluded arrangements, as necessary;

—bring about assistance, transfer of technology and management skills to developing countries on equitable and favourable terms;

—regulate the repatriation of profits accruing from TNE operations, taking into account the legitimate interest of all parties concerned;

—promote reinvestment of TNE profits in developing countries.

The Charter of Economic Rights and Duties of States refers, in Chapter II, to the issue of control over TNEs and draws in this context attention to certain principles of international law such as national sovereignty, territorial integrity, and political independence. On the other hand, as has been explained above, it denies the existence of established principles of public international law governing compensation for nationalization of foreign property and refers exclusively to the law of the nationalising state. Chapter II, Article 2 reads:

> Each State has the right ... to nationalise, expropriate or transfer ownership of foreign property, in which case appropriate compensation should be paid by the State adopting such measures, taking into account its relevant laws and regulations ... where the question of compensation gives rise to a controversy, it shall be settled under the domestic law of the nationalising State ...

These postulates and principles have been interpreted and discussed in countless committees, conferences, seminars, books and articles, speeches and discussion papers, in and outside the various institutions of the U.N. Most of these discussions, however, have not clarified the pertinent issues but have only added to confusion. There are two major reasons for this embroilment:

—there is no general world-wide agreement on the fundamentals of a possible course of action designed to improve international economic relations and to establish a new international economic system;

—the work done so far on the theory of international direct investment does not yet allow the drawing of "final" conclusions about the determinants of investment decisions by TNEs and the impact of TNE activities on the development of the different groups of countries.

Notably the demands and statements from Third World quarters on the issues pertaining to the role of TNEs in a "new international economic order" which have become known hitherto are often vague or even contradictory; this precisely reflects the fact that the instruments adopted in the U.N. framework on this subject represent a political compromise and that the real effects of direct investments are judged on a case-by-case basis and are often assessed in diametrically opposed ways.

2.1.3. *Legal aspects of the instruments postulating a new international economic order*

Some consideration should be given to the legal nature[13] of the instruments containing the demand for a new international economic order.

The Declaration and the Programme of Action were adopted by the U.N. General Assembly by consensus without formal vote. Taking into account their legal basis (Articles 10 and 13 of the U.N. Charter), their wording (cf. Section 4 of the Declaration: "... should be founded on the following principles ..."), and their context, they represent non-binding recommendations with programmatic goals. One might, on the other hand, argue that their moral and political significance is very high. The legal significance (cf. Section 7 of the Declaration: "The present declaration ... shall be one of the most important bases of economic relations between all peoples and all nations") was, however, considerably reduced by the supplementary statements and reservations of 38 countries[14] made right after the "adoption" of the Declaration and Programme of Action.

By contrast, the Charter was conceived of by its initiators as an instrument for the codification and progressive development of international law. This attempt to convert the prospective new international economic order into a legally-binding system of new economic rights and duties of states was, however, rejected by OECD countries and failed to achieve its object. After the rejection of an application by the EC states to continue the comparatively brief negotiations of the respective working group until a universally-acceptable formulation of the Charter could be found, six OECD States (Belgium, Denmark, the Federal Republic of Germany, Great Britain, Luxembourg, U.S.A.) voted against the adoption of the Charter while ten market-economy industrial nations (Austria, Canada, France, Ireland, Israel, Italy, Japan, the Netherlands, Norway, Spain) abstained.

This rejection of the Charter by OECD nations, the TNEs and business enterprises of which control more than 70 per cent of the world market, has resulted in poor chances for the early realization of the "new international economic order" in international economic relations, especially as the oil and currency crisis have — notwithstanding the immense dangers implicit in the energy situation — so far been successfully managed and the OECD countries seem, therefore, to believe that they are under less pressure to support reforms. Nevertheless, the fact remains that the passage of these instruments is a victory for the South.

The fact that these General Assembly Resolutions are not legally binding[15] does not preclude the possibility of certain legal effects resulting from the Charter: as in the case of other U.N. Resolutions, the Charter has been cited as a legal argument in international judicial and state practice.[16] It should also be kept in mind that in economic conflicts between states and in international economic diplomacy, international relations are, in principle, not viewed from a purely juridical angle, but are widely open to economic considerations and interests.

The legal effects of the Charter can be seen in the use of the Charter's rules in state practice, especially of those articles which were adopted unanimously in the vote of the second Committee of the U.N. General Assembly and which lay the basis for new legal standards and principles. Also, the discussions and voting can have prejudicial value for the determination of rules of international law. [17] Thus for instance, many developing countries infer from the vote on Article 2, paragraph 2(c) of the Charter (104:16:6) rejecting the "classical" international minimum standard, in the case of expropriation of foreign investments that, in view of the many contradictions in state practice and doctrine, it is not possible to prove the existence of international customary law restrictions on the sovereign right to nationalise foreign property, and that an international law obligation for the "full, prompt and effective" compensation of nationalized foreign property is not recognized in most developing countries.

Thus, the possible legal effects have to be examined separately for each individual provision of the Charter and depend, inter alia, on the votes, wording and interrelationships of the individual articles of the respective instruments, on existing international law, and future state practice. The *opinio* juris and legal practice of OECD states seems to be of particular importance as it is actually to them that most of the obligations are addressed. As recognized in the jurisprudence of the International Court of Justice, universal international law cannot be created against the will of an entire group of states; the will of the individual states most affected does play a decisive role. [18]

Hence, as already mentioned, the importance of the following sentence contained in the OECD Guidelines for Multinational Enterprises: [19] "OECD Member countries set forth the ... Guidelines for Multinational Enterprises with the understanding that Member countries will fulfil their responsibilities to treat enterprises equitably and in accordance with international law and international agreements, as well as contractual obligations to which they have subscribed". The reference to international law may concern particularly the protection of foreign property, i.e., the amount and modalities of compensation in cases of nationalisation. The sentence referred to has, like the whole set of guidelines, no binding force, but it may legally be qualified as an attempt to restate the law concerning the protection of foreign property in a period of rapid change. [20]

There are clear indications that the structure of international law is changing. International lawyers, [21] notably also in the OECD states, have, for some time, emphasised the need to supplement the international "law of coexistence" by an international "law of cooperation" and have analyzed and supported the gradual emergence of a new "international economic development law", a *"droit international du développement"* ideally within the framework of realistic and effective U.N. development strategies. Another major aspect of such a prospective international law of cooperation would be that the problems arising from world economic and political interdependence, from the exhaustibility of certain resources, and from environmental pollution, can, to a large extent, be solved effectively only by global cooperation (instead of unilateral national measures) and that to this end certain legal limitations on state sovereignty in favour of international cooperation are essential. The development of such a new international law requires a global political understanding on the fundamentals of a new international economic system.

2.1.4. *Political and ideological aspects of the demand for a "new international economic order"*

The following short dialogue written by Carl Sandburg might illustrate certain aspects of the fundamental issues at stake:

"Get off this estate".
"What for?"
"Because it's mine".
"Where did you get it?"

"From my father".
"Where did he get it?"
"From his father".
"And where did he get it?"

"He fought for it".

"Well, I'll fight you for it".

By describing North-South disputes concerning economic issues as a struggle over the distribution of wealth, many northern analysts assimilate them into a familiar form of social conflict. There is certainly merit in this analysis which, in an analogy to the social struggle of the working class during the second half of the last century, describes the North-South problem as the great social question of the last two decades of this century. But this analysis may contain only part of the truth. If nothing more were at stake, one would anticipate, for instance, defections from the southern bloc, particularly on an issue like oil prices. If, however, one returns to the "conception of anticolonialism as the Third World élite's deeply emotional response to a sense of humiliation", [22] then the solidarity of "the 77" ceases to be surprising. Though the spokesmen of the South are familiar with the thinking and the value systems of the North, i.e., the Western industrialised countries (and are sometimes products of such systems by privileged education) they know nevertheless — as Farer explains in a rather convincing way — that they are leaders of countries once alleged by Western scholars and diplomats to be incapable of participating in the international legal system because they were not "civilised states". For hundreds of years they have been people to whom things happen.

Thus, for instance, the close-to-universal support for OPEC is a clear sign of the subordination of economic interests to ideological preoccupations. This was very well demonstrated during the Paris Conference on International Economic Cooperation (CIEC) what the West envisaged as a "trilateral" conference of industrial countries, oil producers and developing countries, was transformed by the developing countries into a bilateral dialogue between themselves on one side and the industrial states on the other. [23] In this respect, the economic political and ideological aspects of the North-South dialogue are inseparably linked. To insist on setting aside the political character of the dialogue can only be seen as "naiveté" or as an attempt at "politicisation" in the most calculating sense of the term. [24]

Another example, also used by Farer, might illustrate the political and ideological aspects of the discussion on the "new international economic order". It brings us back to the problem of "expropriation", which is directly related to the subject of this study: what are the reasons for the incessant campaign against the obligation, enshrined in the classical system on international law, to compensate the alien owners of expropriated property (according to a "prompt, adequate, and effective" standard), despite new phenomena in this field concerning both recent developments in international law, which have been explained above, and actual host country behaviour, centering notably on methods for evaluating expropriated enterprises and renegotiation in certain cases, which have opened the door to compromise?

The Third World élites know, Farer says, that, like the idea of freedom and human rights, the sanctity of property is a major facet of the West's creed; hence they must be fairly confident that they will not obtain the acknowledgement they seek; they also know that nationalisation of foreign enterprises without compensation is — though there *are* well-known cases — comparatively rare in the legal practice of most developing countries anxious to maintain a good investment climate. Whatever the international legal standard may be, private capital will not flow to states ruled by régimes with a penchant for confiscation. In addition, in most cases, compensation may be only marginally relevant to the distribution of wealth. If, nevertheless, the southern bloc is waging a campaign which it cannot hope to win, its persistence must reflect something more than a set of shrewdly calculated economic claims. What it does reflect is the claim to autonomy, to insulation from appraisal by the governments of Western states. [25]

These fundamental political and ideological aspects should be kept in mind if one is to understand the South's plea for a "new international economic order". If the West does not understand these important psychological and ideological components of the North-South dialogue (or confrontation), it will be much easier for the Communist world to strengthen its influence in the South; there is a lot of Marxist ideology in the pertinent discussions and deliberations on the concept of a "new international economic order", in particular regarding the issues pertaining to the activities of TNEs. Commercial activities are, for instance, defined as "exploitation"; this proposition follows directly from Marxist thinking that any net income not going to wages is "surplus value"; it is also alleged *ad nauseam* that under colonialism the instruments of exploitation were the colonial administration and under "neo-colonialism" they are the modern TNEs.

2.1.5. *The skeptics' view*

The establishment of a "new international economic order" as described by the U.N. General Assembly has become the major objective of the developing countries, supported at least rhetorically by the industrialised socialist nations. Several developed market economies such as the Netherlands and the Scandinavian group give political support to the concept. In the other industrialised countries important groups are in favour of changes in the world economy aimed at improving the position and prospects of the developing world.

There are, naturally, important voices in the industrial countries that question the basic idea of a "new international economic order", On principle, the skeptics point to the need to rebut a political offensive. Irving Kristol, for example, has written: "In truth the 'new cold war' is not really about economics at all, but about politics. At bottom is a conflict of political ideologies. What the Third World is saying is not that it needs our help but that their poverty is the fault of our capitalism ..." [26] It is argued with considerable logic by the skeptics of a "new international economic order" that the principal cause for the Third World's poverty is not external but internal. [27]

The skeptics point also to the obvious contradiction in the rhetoric of certain spokesmen from developing countries who describe their cause as just and humane, and at the same time, subject their people to a widespread deprivation of human rights and to economic oppression. Charles Ries underlines this as a powerful argument since the most important motivation in the North for assistance to developing countries is the basic concern for the material condition of the people of the Third World — and not its governments. Where the leaders of developing countries for quite understandable reasons emphasise the state as the moral unit entitled to sovereign equality, freedom, and equal chance for economic success, "the developed countries are likely to see the poor and deprived Third World peasant as the object of special assistance." [28]

A second major philosophical basis for objection to the "new international economic order" has been that many aspects of the proposal of the "Group of 77" involve a limitation or abolition of the market-based system of international economic exchanges. The classical contention is that open markets are the most efficient allocators of scarce resources and the best guarantors of human freedom. These arguments acknowledge, of course, only rarely that many governments already tend to limit the free play of markets by different means and that what is actually at stake is the relative intervention and management of markets.

Most objections to the "new international economic order" are practical and based on pragmatic grounds and normally focus on critical arguments against the demands for an integrated programme for commodity trade, including the indexation of commodity prices to world inflation levels, the Special Drawing Right (SDR)-development "link", agreement to a date for the achievement of the 0.7 per cent of GNP official development assistance (ODA) target and the provisions pertaining to industrialization, including technology transfer, restrictive business practices, and TNE issues. [29]

2.1.6. *"Inner limits"*

So far the West's attitude in the North-South dialogue has not been very convincing. There is, in fact, not even a real North-South dialogue aimed at doing away with existing imbalances. Only the South has defined its posture. The northern democracies instead seem committed to a policy of status quo-ism, aimed at averting change by delaying actions. And the socialist countries try to keep away from any meaningful negotiations, as if the reordering of the world systems and the financial contributions for the improvement of the material condition of the people in developing countries were none of their business.

The situation is illustrated by the work of the U.N. Committee of the Whole, [30] designed to overview progress in the process towards a new international economic system, which was obliged to temporarily suspend its activities in September 1978. The reason was that several industrial countries objected to the proposal of the developing world that the mandate of the committee should include reference to its ability to negotiate the issues. The "Group of 77" ultimately modified the proposal to: "... the Committee will negotiate with a view to its adopting guidelines on central policy sissues ...". This version was also turned down and a few days later the representatives of 150 U.N. member states went home. Towards the end of 1978 this text was finally accepted. In the meanwhile, prestige and precious momentum had been lost. This is a good example for the "inner limits" which constrain our capacity to reshape the world order. [31]

There are, as Peccei and Laszlo explain, "inner limits" of ignorance, superficial information flows, and irresponsible "what-can-I-do-about-it-anyway?" attitudes. Yet, the governments of the industrial countries will not act unless public concern increases dramatically. Public concern, however, is unlikely as long as the fundamental issues are not better understood. Somebody somewhere must "... take the first step to break the vicious circle which still confines mankind within these inner limits to the human growth," [32] which is the crucial condition for the solution of today's world problems.

In the same vein there is yet another reason for the slow progress towards a new international system: the lack of a holistic approach designed to understand contemporary problems and to discover solutions. Most scientific and socio-political research and teaching (and most politicians and decisionmakers have been taught to operate in that way during their student years) removes obstacles here and there or casts light into some hidden corners, which might indeed be very useful but does not reveal what is most important, i.e., the direction and potential of the course in which modern life is caught up. Love of detail and the ability to bring it to the forefront often obscure the wider context. One of the imbalances of modern society is produced by its large supply of specialists and analysts and the lack instead of synthetizers and integrators. [33]

2.2. *Elements of a new international economic system*

While emphasising the need for an intrinsic understanding of the attitudes taken by the spokesmen of the South and the largest possible degree of openness toward the South's needs, the author of this study is neither of the opinion that the West should feel "guilty" nor that all the demands advanced by the South should be accepted. The study defends, however, the position that the West does — notably because of its strength and potential — have a moral duty and also a great direct interest to develop, in cooperation with the South, a global strategy in order to be responsive to the basic demands of the South and to take the lead in the process of reshaping the international economic system.

The question of the direction and the degree of change is, of course, the major point of discussion. Because of the West's still formidable wealth of knowledge, experience, and intellectual and material resources, it should, to begin with, now enunciate the responsibilities which Western industrialised countries will have to bear in this process toward a new international economic system.

To be effective the new international economic system must be responsive to both the problems confronting the developing countries as well as to the difficulties of developed countries in the present state of the world economy.

The new international economic system is, however, part of a more comprehensive process which should lead to a new equitable world order of peace. What the developing countries really demand is not merely an increased participation in economic benefits but a fundamental redistribution of political power.

2.2.1. *Disarmament*

The first and most basic prerequisite for a new global system of peace is the conclusion and effective implementation of disarmament agreements. The present arms race is incompatible with the quest for a new political system of peace and it seriously hampers the material possibilities for achieving a new international economic system.

2.2.2. *Basic needs*

The attainment of the official development aid objective of 0.7 per cent of GNP is essential. In the low-income developing countries this aid must be used to strengthen the rural infrastructure in order to increase agricultural productivity. Aid must help meet the basic needs of the majority of the people who are very poor. These needs are more and better food, safe water at hand, security of livelihood, health, sanitation, education, decent shelter, adequate transport; in addition, there are "non-material" needs [34] like self-confidence, self-reliance, dignity, capacity to make one's own decisions, to participate in the decisions that affect one's life and work, and to develop one's talents, all of which interact in a variety of ways with "material" needs.

Meeting the basic needs of the millions of very poor people requires changes not only in income distribution but also in the structure of production. Efforts must be made to develop efficient labour-intensive technologies, i.e., technologies that economize in the use of capital and sophisticated skills and management, and are appropriate for the social, cultural, and climatic conditions of developing countries, especially in farming, processing, and agro-business, as well as for exports and for import substitution.

2.2.3. *Trade*

As to the middle-income developing countries, where development depends more on international trade and capital markets, a significant improvement in the terms of trade of these countries and easier access for their export products to the markets of the industrialized countries is necessary.

The industrial countries should encourage operation of market forces and the development of world trade. For this purpose, trade restrictions should be removed on industrial countries' imports of textiles, clothing, shoes, processed foods, and many other manufactured articles, in which areas the poor countries are able to develop their productive capacity. The domestic adjustment in industrial countries made necessary by the removal of such trade barriers should be facilitated through adjustment finance.

On the other hand — and this aspect will become still more important in the future — it should be recognised that the advantages of free trade between states at widely differing levels of development are often on the side of the industrialised country. As Friedrich List observes already in his "Outlines of American Political Economy," [35] written at the beginning of the 19th century and concerned with a striking parallel to the present North-South controversy, i.e., the political-economic conflict between the U.S.A., a weak ex-colonial state and England, the world power of that time: "The old country ... will in a free intercourse ever keep down a rising manufacturing power."

Thus, an overly-rigid adherence to the doctrine of free trade might be counterproductive in commercial relations with developing countries. The theory of free trade as formulated by the classical economists (Adam Smith and Ricardo) and perfected by the neo-classicists (Haberler, Hecksher, and Ohlin) states that in an economic universe where the means of production are not mobile, international division of labour based on the principle of "comparative advantage" leads to a higher global production of all goods than would be achieved in the absence of this division of labour, and in this manner, not only the world community but each nation individually benefits. In opposition to this, the theorists of imperialism (e.g., François Perroux, John K. Galbraith and Joan Robinson) point out, as did Friedrich List, that free trade favours the domination of the strong over the weak country by tilting the terms of trade to the benefit of the former and by blocking the possibility of technological development by the latter. Some claim that Japan owes her economic development to the protectionism she has maintained. In any event, it is clear that technology, labour, and capital are far more mobile today than in the old days and that the "problem of choosing between free trade and protectionism cannot be limited to the question of the exchange of goods." [36]

As already explained in the introduction to this study, high interdependence between nations which are only slightly integrated politically may be a dangerous phenomenon, in particular for the economically weaker country; in part for this reason, Keynes was sympathetic to protectionism in his "General Theory" [37] Today, many people begin to advocate an "organised liberalism" to smooth, inter alia, the adoption which will be induced by the developing countries' industrialisation. The question is if this *"libéralisme organisé"* will be designed in favour of the developing countries or in favour of developed countries.

In the author's view, while maintaining a genuine liberal free market system, certain developing countries should, under certain conditions, have the possibilities to make unilateral derogations to the general principle of free trade in order to protect certain industries. These derogations should be of a limited and temporary nature; their need must be re-examined periodically in the framework of a multilateral forum.

One might also consider the proposition of maintaining free trade within zones seeking integration (i.e., for instance, the EC or the OECD countries or certain groups of developing countries) but of defining *between* these various zones a more flexible relationship, taking into account varying degrees of development and the disparity of objectives.

2.2.4. *Commodities*

Another issue-oriented approach in the framework of a new international economic system must embrace the problem of commodities, i.e., the establishment of an international agreement on commodities assuring equitable and remunerative income for developing countries' exports. Considerable progress has been made in the Geneva negotiations preceding the UNCTAD V meeting in Manila. Both producers and consumers (developed and developing countries are found on both sides of the fence) have parallel interests in reducing market instability and in the long-run growth of economic supply in line with sustainable global economic growth. The Lomé agreement might be used as a model for export revenue stabilisation.

2.2.5. *Selective debt relief*

A further element in an international system of economic security, taking into account the needs of developing countries, should be the adoption of principles for dealing with the burden of *external indebtedness* which has become a major constraint on the economic progress of a large number of developing countries. At the same time, there might be a need for improvement of existing institutions and procedures through which long-term funds are channelled.

Some observers think that selective debt relief might have a detrimental effect on the creditworthiness of developing countries; the respective countries may, however, avoid this negative impact by exposing their economic policy to international scrutiny (e.g., by the IMF).

2.2.6. *Monetary stability*

Monetary stability would be another facet of a new international economic system. It is unfortunately true that since the widespread adoption of floating exchange rates, the momentum for the reform of the international monetary system has been very largely lost. In the short-run, there may be a certain amount of satisfaction with floating exchange rates. Instability of exchange rates prevents, however, longer-term planning on the part of exporting enterprises. Erratic fluctuations and the decline of the value endanger certain industries, without this having anything to do with the laws of competition. In addition, the rate of inflation is rising in those countries where the value of the currency is declining, without inflation rates being considerably reduced where the value of the currency is rising. [38] The New European Monetary System is an important step towards monetary stability, but there is an immediate need for progress in a much wider framework.

2.2.7. *Energy*

Recent increases in oil prices have disastrous effects on most non-OPEC developing countries. These countries need special help in their efforts to decrease their dependency on oil products. They must develop alternative sources of energy (e.g., solar energy, coal and biomass) but at the same time avoid destroying the ecological equilibrium (e.g., the problem of erosion of land due to over-consumption of wood).

OPEC countries should to some extent be prepared to grant preferential price treatment to non-oil-developing countries. Political considerations might promote this objective. UNCTAD V provides some indication in this direction.

The process towards a new international economic system would require that the production of energy be more widely and evenly distributed and that scarcities be avoided. New sources must be discovered requiring huge investments in expensive alternative technologies, with great uncertainties and long time lags.

There is a need for an international energy strategy to balance supply and demand of oil in a context of stringent conservation. The adoption and implementation of such a strategy would help solving the world's energy problems by peaceful means.

TNE's may have to play a decisive role in the process of world-wide restructuring of energy resources. Governments of developed and developing countries must take, in time, the steps necessary for a smooth transition to a new energy economy.

2.2.8. *International organisations*

The governments of industrial countries should continue to support the operation of *international organizations* such as the IMF, the World Bank and GATT, which are designed to internalise the global negative externalities arising from the operation of free market forces, taking into account the special needs of developing countries. Thus, developing countries should enjoy — to the extent that this serves both their economic development and effective international economic cooperation — special concessions and preferential treatment.

Industrialised countries must, to some extent, waive their claims to enforcing the principle of mutuality. This would mean that for the rights and obligations of countries participating in the new international economic system a "double standard" would be introduced, putting certain developing countries in a privileged position to the extent that they are disadvantaged; this would partly compensate for their inferior condition. This is the price which the industrial countries will have to pay in order to "buy" the developing countries' adherence to a basically still liberal free market system.

There are undoubted world benefits from the past activities undertaken by the IMF, the development efforts of the World Bank, and the work of GATT. The recognition of the right of developing countries to play their proper role in all international negotiations is, however, essential in this context.

The proposed framework does not require the removal of the existing system and structure. The objective is to ensure the survival of the system by lessening or eliminating unacceptable consequences.

UNCTAD and other U.N. organisations will play a major role in the continuing process of international negotiations, notably in the field of commodities, transfer of technology, restrictive business practices, industrialisation, technical cooperation among developing countries, food production and distribution, energy and ores, environmental problems, issues pertaining to the ocean management, and the problems of armaments reduction.

2.2.9. *The proper level of decision-making*

Finally, there is the issue of the proper level of initiative, consultation, negotiation, and decision-making. A new international economic system, while introducing certain nuances which have been outlined above, must retain the fundamental principles of economic liberalism. Decentralisation as a fundamental principle must be emphasised. Such a philosophy is responsive to the desire and needs of the individual human beings who wish to participate in the decisions which affect their present and future welfare. Such a philosophy defends, develops, and reinforces, in the main, an economic system which rewards the essential virtues of a free enterprise system, such as investment, innovation, and notably the willingness to take a personal economic risk. No one has pointed out in a more convincing way how vital the preservation of these virtues is than Adam Smith in *The Wealth of Nations.* [39] Without these virtues the world's productivity will decline, an undesirable development implying detrimental consequences for the North and even worse for the South.

On the other hand, the review of the present socio-economic and political difficulties undertaken in section 1 of this Chapter has shown that there are limits to the effectiveness of decentralised activities. Thus, a certain amount of centralisation is necessary to ensure optimum welfare through the acceleration of a process towards a new international economic system. The criterion, which determines when centralisation is part of the optimum decision process, is whether lower-level decisions have significant effects on outsiders.

It is obvious that the decisions made by governments, inter-governmental institutions, or business organisations, as, for instance, the TNEs, which affect the course of the process towards a new international economic system and thus imply by definition "external effects", will have to be made at level suited to the designing of a world economic policy. Ideally, this task would be the function of a world government or at least of an efficient international political superstructure.

Needless to say, the present "superstructure" composed by 150 sovereign states acting under the rule of the one-state, one-vote principle, and a considerable number of TNEs cannot be an efficient organisational framework for dealing with the issues pertaining to the new international economic system. No one is really in charge and feels responsible for the whole.

It might, therefore, be worthwhile to consider favourably Tinbergen's [40] proposal to establish a council or several councils comprising ten to fifteen members representing the different regions of the world. [41] The people sitting in these councils might be drawn from the world-wide "club" of statesmen, multilateral conference diplomats, TNE top managers or international trade union leaders; this under two conditions: first in addition to their experience in the tactics of the international political and economic game they must distinguish themselves by a profound knowledge of the subjects at hand, a synthesizing brain, and vision; they must be convincing personalities, deeply rooted in their own local cultures and regions and, at the same time, they must be at the crossroads of the world's cultural developments and have the minds of world statesmen. Second, to be credible and effective such a "council" would need a democratic basis. The members of the "council" or "board" should therefore each be elected by the parliaments, e.g. the democratic or "quasi-democratic representations" in the different states of their respective regions. The details of this proposal would, of course, need further elaboration.

It is likely that the political prerequisites for such councils cannot be created in the foreseeable future as this would require the surrender of certain sovereign rights by states to a higher level of authority. Notably the Communist-ruled regions would not, at present, be willing to join such a world superstructure. The Western industrialised democracies would also hesitate. And the developing countries would not join because they particularly emphasise their sovereign status.

Although there is a little chance of implementing the above model in the present political reality, the concept of such "councils" for consultation and strengthening of cooperation" or of a "world development board" or "authority" should be pursued further at the appropriate time.

The idea of such a "world development board" is not a revolutionary concept. The local, national, and transnational enterprises, the respective trade unions and interest groups, the cultural entities and religious groups and organisations, the local communities, provinces, states and regional and multi-regional organisations would continue to play their role and assume their proper tasks and responsibilities.

The world development board composed of "world statesmen" would monitor the work of the international organisations.

In view of the growing dissatisfaction this would be also a fitting occasion to review the operations of these international organisations and to make the necessary improvements. The organisations would, after this adjustment, continue their work under the auspices of the new "board". Thus, from a functional point of view, the "world development board" could be compared with the highest "surveillance"-entity of a very decentralised "geocentric TNE". The final objective of such a prospective world development board would be — while avoiding all sorts of costly administrative machinery or of dirigistic interference with subsectoral processes or specific cases — to monitor, supervise and direct the general process leading towards an improved international economic system.

In the short run, however, it might be necessary to envisage a more realistic and practicable solution, which would be based on the actual distribution of political and economic power: the creation of a World Security Council for Economic Questions. World economic problems are, indeed, so profound, that their solution has to be sought together with the settlement of political issues. On the other hand we must not allow political crises to be settled at the cost and to the detriment of vital economic questions. Hence the need for an international forum for discussing and monitoring problems of economic security.[42]

2.3. *The process*

It was already pointed out at the beginning of this chapter that the process leading to the establishment of a new international economic system will not be necessarily harmonious and peaceful. This is because, once the process of redistribution of the social pie starts, no group is willing to settle for less, when it believes it could have more. Thus, confrontation and struggle over the allocation of wealth and structural power seem endemic.

There will be a thorny sequence of confrontations and negotiations leading, hopefully, to particular forms of cooperation; the latter will be promoted by the fear that everybody will lose if the process becomes counterproductive as a result of self-defeating competition and confrontation. But there might be, nevertheless, years of bitter conflict ahead.

Like in all class struggles and revolutionary developments in history, the initiative is with the weaker party, which is the "demandeur" and produces new ideas designed to "entangle" the minds of the ruling groups. It has been shown, therefore, in this chapter that the process toward establishing a new international economic system has, in addition to its economic and political component, also an important ideological facet.

It is in the long-term interest of the industrialised countries to find ways of favouring the developing countries' development, while minimising the unfavourable impacts of this development process on their own situation, in order to limit potential social unrest in their areas as far as possible. The people in the West will, to some extent, have to make some important material sacrifices; this might help them to find new life styles and new attitudes towards their environment, which will anyway be required in any case in view of possible shortages and crises (such as energy) which might already occur before the end of this century. Though the process of world development is likely to be accompanied by social and political clashes, the difficulties might be still greater if this process were delayed.

The attitude of the West should not be entirely based on shortsighted tactical considerations. There is more involved. A far-sighted strategy is needed. Because of its basic commitment to political and economic freedom and to the dignity of man, which still is the West's creed and, as such, part of the common heritage of mankind, because of its economic strength and moral potential, the West must be responsive to today's planetary challenges for world development and now take the lead in accelerating the process of rethinking and reshaping the bases of the international system.

This is not to say that the West should alone bear the economic and financial burden of the adjustment process. Other regions will have to join: for instance, the Eastern countries and the very advanced developing countries. The OPEC countries which create enormous difficulties to many developing countries by their oil price policy must continue to strengthen their development efforts.

One important element of the process leading to a new international economic system needs further exploration: the issues pertaining to a framework for international investment and the activities of TNEs. This is the subject of the following chapter.

Notes to chapter six

1. Van Lennep, Emile, "New Approaches to International Cooperation in a Changing and Interdependent World", *The Atlantic Community Quarterly*, p. 358-368 (1977).

2. See also Grant James, "Central Issues in the North-South Dialogue," *OECD Observer*, no. 96, p. 3 (1979).

3. Several speakers mentioned this idea at the occasion of a symposium which was jointly organized by the Parliamentary Assembly of the Council of Europe and OECD in December, 1978.

4. See, e.g., Club of Rome, *Reshaping the International Order* (RIO Report), Tinbergen, Coordinator, N.Y. 1976; Forrester, "Counter-intuitive Behaviour of Social Systems," *Technology Review*, January 1971.

5. See World Bank, *World Development Report*, 1978; the following section draws heavily on this report.

6. World Bank, *World Development Report*, op. cit., p. 68.

7. See Chapter Four, section 2.2 above.

8. Schwarzenberger, *Economic World Order*, 1970, p. 68.

9. See note 38 in Chapter Five.

10. Some recent contributions (e.g., Cohen, *World Money Order*, 1978) distinguish between "structure power" (the ability to set the rules of the game) and "process power" (the ability to use the existing rules to advantage).

11. Jackson, *The Crumbling Institutions of the Liberal Trade System*, Journal of World Trade Law, 1978, p. 93.

12. See U.N. General Assembly, A/RES/3201(S-VI) of 9 May 1974; A/RES/3202(S-VI) of 16 May 1974; and A/RES/3281(XXIX) of 15 January 1975.

13. See Tomuschat, Christian, *Die Charta der wirtschaftlichen Rechte und Pflichten der Staaten*, Zeitschrift für ausländisches öffentliches Recht und Völkerrecht, vol. 36, pp. 444-491 (1976); Petersmann, Ernst U., *International Economic Development Law: Myth or Reality?* Law and State, vol. 15, pp. 7-37 (1977)

14. As evidenced in an arbitration award of 19 January 1977, on

Libya's nationalization of oil concessions of American oil companies, see Journal de Droit International 1977, pp. 319, 350, 377.

15. In international law literature and state practice it is almost unanimously agreed that, because of the wording and systematics of Article 10 et seq. of the U.N. Charter and of the sources of international law as specified in Article 38 of the ICJ Statute, resolutions of the General Assembly establish legal obligations only in a few exceptional cases (e.g., international organizational decisions, termination of the mandate in Southwest Africa/Namibia) and irrespective of their designation ("charter"), are legally non-binding on the subjects to which they are addressed; cf. Tomuschat, op.cit., pp. 466-484; cf. also Seidl-Hohenveldern, *Die "Charta" der wirtschaftlichen Rechte und Pflichten der Staaten*, Recht der internationalen Wirtschaft, 1975, pp. 237 seq.

16. E.g., the above-mentioned arbitration award; see note 14 in this chapter.

17. See Feuer, *Réflexions sur la Charte des Droits et Devoirs Economiques des Etats*, Rev. Générale de Droit International Public (Vol. 79), pp. 274-320 (1975); Petersmann, "International Law and the New International Economic Order," *Deutsche öffentlichrechtliche Landesberichte*, Tübingen 1978, pp. 31-47.

18. See the Continental Shelf Judgement of 20 February 1969, *ICJ Reports* 1969, pp. 4,43.

19. See note 15 in Chapter Two.

20. See Grewlich, *Direct Investment in the OECD Countries*, 1978, p. 94.

21. Cf. for instance, Friedmann, *The Changing Structure of International Law*, 1964, p. 176; "Pays en voie de développement et transformation du droit international," *Colloque de la Société Française pour le droit international* (1974); Petersmann, International Economic Development Law, op.cit.

22. Farer, "The United States and the Third World: A Basis for Accommodation," in *Foreign Affairs*, vol. 54, p. 79, 83 (1975); the following draws to some extent on this paper.

23. See Wessels, Introduction to *Europe and the North-South Dialogue*, 1978.

24. Elmandjra, "Political Facets of the North-South Dialogue," *Forum for Correspondence and Contact*, vol. 10, V-71 (1978).

25. See Farer, op.cit., p. 84.

26. Kristol, "The New Cold War," *Wall Street Journal*, 17 July 1975.

27. Moynihan, "The United States in Opposition," *Commentary 59* (March 1975), pp. 31-44.

28. Ries, "The New International Economic Order: The Skeptics' Views," in Sauvant and Hasenpflug, *The New International Economic Order*, Boulder 1977.

29. See Grubel, "The Case against the New International Economic Order," *Weltwirtschaftliches Archiv* (vol. 113), pp. 284-307 (1977); Bauer and Yamey, "Against the New Economic Order," *Commentary*, April 1977, pp. 25-31.

30. This committee which, in accordance with its mandate, "shall meet, as and when required until the special session of the General Assembly in 1980 dealing with a new international development strategy for the 1980s" assists the General Assembly by acting as a focal point, inter alia, in "overseeing and monitoring the implementation of decisions and agreements reached in the negotiations on the establishment of the new international economic order in the appropriate bodies of the U.N.", cf. General Assembly Resolution 32/174 of 19 December 1977, adopted without a vote.

31. Laszlo, "The Inner Limits to Growth," *Forum for Correspondence and Contact*, V-67 (1979); Peccei, *The Human Quality*, 1977.

32. See note 31.

33. Peccei, *The Human Quality*, 1977.

34. Streeten, "Development Ideas in Historical Perspectives," *Internationales Asienforum*, 1979, pp. 27-40.

35. List, "Outlines of American Political Economy," in List, *Schriften/Reden/Briefe*, vol. II, Berlin 1931; see also Garbe, "Friedrich List and His Relevance for Development Policy," *Intereconomics* pp. 251-256 (1977).

36. Montbrial, "For a New World Economic Order", *Foreign Affairs* (vol. 75), pp. 61-78 (1975).

37. Keynes, *The General Theory of Employment, Interest and Money*, 1936.

38. Montbrial, op.cit., p. 64.

39. Smith (Adam), *The Wealth of Nations*, 5th ed., London, 1789.

40. Tinbergen, "The Need for an Ambitious Innovation of the World Order," *Journal of International Affairs* (vol. 31), pp. 305-314.

41. The Independent Commission on International Development Issues (Brandt Commission), having the limited task of issuing a report (of what is politically feasible in international development) by 1979/80, might be, in its composition, a first precursor of such councils.

42. Such a proposal has been made for instance by Guido Brunner, member of the Commission of the EC, in a speech delivered before "The German Foreign Policy Society" in Bonn on 22 January 1980.

Chapter Seven

A WORLD-WIDE FRAMEWORK FOR DIRECT INVESTMENT AND TRANSNATIONAL ENTERPRISES

What is the proper role of international investment and of TNE activities in a new economic system? What sort of framework would allow TNEs to play an optimal role in the process leading to the new system? The international discussion on this question reflects the varying interests of the different nations; and, as in similar areas of international economic politics, there is as yet no consensus among the nations of the world regarding the details of a practical international action programme which might encompass a comprehensive set of effective world-wide standards for international investment and TNE activities.

The nations of the world are engaged in a continuous international dialogue on the vital aspects of a new economic system. The understanding of what is really going on usually lags to a considerable degree behind the rapid change of circumstances. Thus, in addition to the well-known tactics of international bargaining, it is precisely this time lag which makes many nations rather reluctant to bind themselves by conventions or agreements without having a clear picture of the future trends of development.

This reluctance applies notably to the sensitive area of international investment as well. There exists, however, in the meantime, some common ground: the most widely held view is that TNEs should stay on the agenda for international action. Obviously not all TNE representatives and politicians are prepared to actively promote a development towards an action-oriented and balanced solution implying rights and obligations for all parties concerned. But the process has begun; pertinent negotiations in different international fora are underway and, particularly in the light of some revelations concerning both corporate[1] and governmental misbehaviour, it is probably impossible and would be politically counterproductive to stop this process.

While the Commission on Transnational Corporations of the U.N. started its work in 1975 in a climate of heavy confrontation, and most member countries of the "Group of 77" have shown a rather reserved attitude in the U.N. framework vis-à-vis the phenomenon of TNEs as such, the position of many developing countries represented in the U.N. Commission is today much more a question of nuance; the Eastern countries, on the other hand, have not changed their official attitude for ideological reasons.

In assessing the international bargaining situation and reflecting on the future role of direct investment in a new international economic system, it should not, of course, be forgotten that in day-to-day practice there exist many successful working relationships between TNEs and developing countries. This circumstance, however, should not lead to the simplistic conclusion drawn by a number of observers that the on-going multilateral discussions are of no real importance because bilateral relations are satisfactory in many cases at present. The truth is that bilateral relationships between TNEs and developing countries are, to some extent, still based on the distribution of political and economic power of the past,[2] while the discussions in the U.N. concern the prospective "redistribution" of political and economic power by changing the status quo. By the establishment of a new economic order the developing world expects to redress the imbalance of bargaining power that they perceive between TNEs and the governments or local enterprises with which TNEs deal, and to promote trade and development goals regardless of whether or not such development could be expected from the operation of the free market. This is the reason for the striking phenomenon in which some developing countries which are reliable partners for day-to-day commercial operations of the TNEs take, nevertheless, a radical stance in the U.N. fora. They transpose their own often dirigistic national economic systems on to the world level. Above all, they are convinced that a high degree of group cohesion is necessary in the power game for the future.

Thus, there are plausible explanations for the lamentable reality of a sharp split in the U.N. fora between the Western industrialised market countries and developing countries on the question of the basic acceptability of the TNEs in their present form, i.e., on the evaluation of the current — real and perceived — socio-economic effects of TNE operations and the conditions for their future activities in developing countries.

Having this in mind, it seems, on the other hand, that most developing countries today share the view that the future international economic system must retain the positive elements of international direct investment, i.e., the characteristics of the international production and contracting, finance and marketing organisation of the TNEs, which should, however, be put into the service of the development process. The developing countries' objective for the future is to maximise the benefits and to minimise the detrimental effects resulting from TNE operations.[3]

Enlarging this view to a global perspective, it may be stated that it would be the objective of a world-wide balanced approach to maximise the positive contributions and to minimise the negative impact of international direct investment to the extent possible for all parties concerned.

There are, therefore, two basic questions which deserve consideration:
—What is the role of international investment and TNE activities in a new economic system?
—What is the proper framework (a set of standards) allowing international investment and TNEs to play this role?

1. The role of international investment and transnational enterprises in a new economic system

There is no agreed theory of international investment and there exist no generally recognised development models against which to judge possible roles of international investment and TNEs in the process towards a new economic system. We are, indeed, left with a number of purely voluntaristic philosophies in this field. Would it therefore be appropriate to postpone all action in this field until a solid statistical and theoretical ground for informed decisions has been established? Such an approach ("paralysis by analysis") would not be practical under existing circumstances; in particular, as the problems at hand are, in many cases, not primarily economic but much more political.

The following consideration may illustrate this: developing countries feel themselves faced with the paradox that they desire local control over their economic development but recognise, at the same time, the need for foreign investment to foster their economic development. To resolve this dilemma, many developing countries continue to accept foreign investment but also want to strengthen their control of foreign business conduct in their countries, because they feel that certain TNE activities affect their sense of economic security. Such policies, designed to control TNEs, lead, in many cases, to political tensions between developing countries, TNEs, and industrialised home countries. It would be risky for the international economic system to let such tensions transgress the critical threshold where the danger of international "investment wars" materializes.

Thus, action is necessary. If the source of tensions is primarily political, possible solutions to the problem must equally be political in character, i.e., there is a need for a negotiated framework for international investment operations which would reflect the result of a reasonable political compromise. Within this framework TNEs could then continue to play a positive role in world economic development.

What should be the role of international investment and TNE activities in this process?

Retaining the fundamental principles of economic liberalism TNEs may play an important complementary role in the industrial development, primarily of middle-income developing countries:[4] (*i*) through a real transfer of resources; (*ii*) through assistance to developing countries in the development of their own managerial and administrative expertise and in the reception and creation of technologies which are most adaptable for use in developing countries; and, (*iii*) through the expansion of productive capacity and employment and the establishment of export markets in accordance with national development plans and export orientations of the respective developing host countries.

In the early stages of industrialisation, developing countries tend to rely heavily on transfer mechanisms, such as foreign private direct investment, that combine technology, capital, skills, marketing, and management in one package, while developing nations with more developed industrial structures will be better positioned to define and contract for their specific technology needs. Already at present the growing sophistication of technology buyers and increased competition among the proliferating suppliers of technology have induced a general tendency toward the more specific, unpackaged forms of technology transfer. The trend has been and will be, however, much slower in high technology industries, such as petrochemicals, motor vehicles, precision machine tools and computers, where developing countries lack the requisite expertise and the sources of supply are few. In this area TNEs, in their traditional form of foreign private direct investment, will also have to perform an important role in the development process in the future.

On the other hand, the role which the industrialised market economies assign to international direct investment in the future is made clear in the OECD Guidelines for Multinational Enterprises.[5] Looking at these guidelines form a global perspective, however, they need some enlargement, completion, and, in certain cases, a shifting of the emphasis. The postulated global perspective comprises, necessarily, the Eastern countries' inward and, to an even greater degree, outward investment and industrial cooperation activities.[6]

It is again not the purpose of this section to go into a detailed discussion and evaluation of the present real and perceived impacts of international direct investment.[7] It is obvious that the undifferentiated radical bias of certain quarters against TNEs in general is unjustified. Certain reports on the subject were too ideological and ignored important evidence and empirical facts; notably, they did not take into account the beneficial effect of many TNE activities in developing countries in view of the actual urgency of developing needs in poor countries and the fact of the relative erosion of foreign aid as a means of development. It should also be clearly understood by the critics of TNEs that, in general, most TNEs can survive if they pull out of developing countries; but the development process in many developing countries would be badly disrupted in this case.[8]

This is not to say that there are no problems which have to be solved in the near future if TNEs are to perform a positive role in the process leading to a new international economic system. There is, for instance, the very basic problem that the style of development fostered by transnational enterprises is not always responsive to the satisfaction of the real needs in developing countries. Inevitably, TNEs have to produce for those who can buy, rather than for those who are in need. Thus, TNEs become linked to and dependent upon the affluent sectors of society because these are the principal consumers. In the short run, TNEs can make no direct contribution to the solution of this problem, i.e., the establishment of a coincidence of production and of the most demanded and the most needed products. This is a matter of the equalisation of the income distribution and requires governmental policies designed to reduce inequality.

This relates to the issues pertaining to the "basic needs approach". As pointed out already, basic needs are primarily a matter for cooperation on the basis of official development aid. TNEs may, to the extent that the commercial character of their activities allows it, contribute only indirectly to the basic needs problem, e.g., by the creation of labour-intensive technologies.

Another fundamental issue is that TNEs have a cultural impact through product and quality choices, together with the marketing methods used, which is far-reaching and may tend to promote a homogeneity in consumption in the different societies where TNEs operate; this may clash with some societies' aspirations toward greater cultural identity and self-assertion. Here again, however, there is a need for clarification and differentiation: there may be virtue in this criticism to the extent that TNEs operate on the basis of artificially-stimulated demand and, in fact, waste, and thus propagate a questionable "cultural" pattern of Western industrialised societies or promote their particular "company culture". On the other hand, it is important to understand the business perspective: if someone is able to produce a good, useful, and cheap product, he fulfils, so to speak, besides all commercial considerations, a moral duty if he makes the product known, brings it to the place where it is needed (or produces it there), and sells it to those who demand it.

Many more problems and criticism exist, most of which have already been mentioned at the end of Part One of this study.[9] The critics' and proponents' views should not be repeated here, except the basic conclusions, that:

—in general, the promotion of the right type of direct investment or contractual arrangements may be a rational means of achieving higher welfare levels in a certain group of developing countries, notably, the middle-income countries;

—informed and responsible criticism of TNEs is not, in most cases, based on the premise that foreign investment is bad, but rather on the assumption that the real benefits to be derived from direct investment operations and TNE activities could still be greater.

One way of achieving the latter objective would be for all concerned parties to agree on a political and socio-economic framework which would allow the TNEs to play an optimal role as a stabilising and powerful instrument for innovation and world economic development in the process leading to a new international economic system.

2.   Standards for direct investment and the activities of transnational enterprises

Even if the U.N. Commission on Transnational Enterprises were able to agree on a code of conduct in the near future — and hopefully this will be possible — the thoughts and considerations contained in the following sections of this study would not become obsolete, as the prospective U.N. code would not — and this is due to the very nature of the subject and the political circumstances prevailing in the process towards achieving a new international economic system [10] — settle all possible major issues once and for all and thus create complete "security of law". The U.N. code would be a first step; it would be a "living document", which should, of course, at present, already have a considerable normative impact and which would therefore create a certain amount of "legal" security, but, at the same time, it would still have a number of lacunae and would thus necessitate the constant continuation of negotiations concerning TNEs as a vital aspect of the dynamics towards achieving a new international economic system. Thus, the U.N. code would not, in fact, be a code in the traditional legal meaning, where a "code" implies "compilation of existing laws, their systematic arrangement ... designed to regulate completely subjects to which they relate." [11]

2.1. *Western countries should take the initiative*

As emphasized in several places in this study, it is the West's moral duty and in her enlightened interest to develop a credible strategy for being responsive to the desperate situation of the people in the poor countries. Such a strategy must be comprehensive and, at the same time, specific and selective, taking into account the particular situation in the different developing countries. Each situation requires a special mix of official aid in its traditional form, the basic needs approach and international investment, including varying contracting arrangements.

Western industrialised countries should do more than merely accept the need to discuss, more or less reluctantly, the issues pertaining to the establishment of a framework for the activities of TNEs. The West should take the initiative in these discussions. Precisely in the field of direct investment, the West has an immediate interest at stake, as most headquarters of the major TNEs are located in the industrialised market economies.

However, there is a more basic reason why the West should

take a constructive and active attitude in the pertinent discussions taking place in the U.N. framework: the deliberations on TNEs in the framework of the U.N., having the objective of formulating a code of conduct, might give to the West the possibility to "codify" world-wide liberal ideas which have shown to be successful in reality. This is a unique chance which the West must seize. [12] The work of the U.N. Commission for Transnational Corporations will have a decisive impact on the nature of the future international economic system, i.e., on the long-term survival of the fundamental principle of economic liberalism.

2.2. *A balanced set of standards*

The representatives of Western market economies should promote the idea of a balanced set of standards for international investment and the activities of TNEs. As to the notion of "standards", these might comprise principles and provisions contained in one single or in separate instruments, such as multilateral agreements and arrangements, codes of conduct, guidelines, etc. The complex legal questions relating to the nature and binding force of possible standards will be discussed in section 2.3 of this chapter.

2.2.1. *Purposes: development, reduction of tensions, economic liberalism*

Such a framework of standards — provided certain limits are not transgressed — might notably serve three vital purposes: TNEs' contributions to development, the reduction of political tensions, and the maintenance of economic liberalism and entrepreneurial freedom.

To serve these objectives, standards for direct investment should encourage TNEs to make possible contributions to the specific development needs in the various countries where they operate (e.g., by making use of labour-intensive technologies, by establishing special training programmes for locals, or by an adequate amount of reinvestment).

A vital reason for the existence of a set of standards is to diminish the potential for tension and conflict inherent in foreign direct investment operations and TNE activities. Tensions arise, inter alia, because TNE activities affect, in certain cases, a country's sense of economic security. [13] This might cause the affected host country to take measures against the TNE or the home country; or, as in the case of investment incentives, home countries may feel obliged to take retaliatory measures against host countries, [14] thus provoking the danger of "investment wars". The standards should help to avoid such problems and therefore contain a number of appropriate provisions to strengthen cooperation between all concerned parties.

Another objective of the standards would be to maintain the necessary degree of economic liberalism and entrepreneurial freedom. The standards should be based on a philosophy which rewards, develops, and reinforces the essential virtues of a free enterprise system, such as investment, innovation, and the will to take a personal economic risk, as these are the basic conditions for sustained economic growth and development. TNEs find themselves harassed by partly unnecessary impediments and restrictions, by complex and conflicting laws, regulations, and administrative practices [15] that may seriously hinder them from making an optimum contribution to the welfare of nations. Under these circumstances, the appropriate action for the world community is the encouragement of reasonable competition through the dismantling of unnecessary national controls and regulations and limiting the establishment of new ones which are not essential for the process leading towards a new international economic system. Thus, to cite an example, an international framework for the harmonization of rules of competition is quite important, taking into account, of course, the special situation of developing countries by providing (in variation of the infant-industry argument) for a number of exceptions to the free play of international market forces.

2.2.2. *World-wide scope*

The scope of standards for direct investment and the activities of TNEs must be world-wide because the phenomenon which necessitates such standards has transnational dimensions. Many nations, therefore, see the United Nations as the cure for their collective weakness in the face of the TNEs. Are such expectancies justified?

It is correct that at present the U.N. would not be in a position to effectively "enforce" such standards because the degree of sovereignty which would have to be sacrificed by individual nations to enforce (binding) standards does not seem to be realistic at a gloval level at present. As the U.N. would thus lack the ability to force all nations to accept such standards, there would be sufficient loopholes to circumvent such international action.

This might be different at the regional level, where nations have similar intersts and greater opportunities for effective, unified action. [16] Regional efforts (e.g., the Andean Common Market or the EEC) are important, [17] and they may, indeed, have greater chances to be successful. Regional efforts might supplement the action on the world level; they cannot, however, substitute for global action on the subject. TNEs are a genuinely global issue, like the environment and the law of the sea. We cannot escape from the necessity to continue the worldwide dialogue which has been started, and we must make an attempt to come, as early as possible, to some reasonable basic principles designed to reduce tensions and to establish a sound framework for further negotiations.

2.2.3. *Balanced approach: addressees and contents of standards*

If the standards are to alleviate tensions between developing countries, TNEs, and industrialized countries and to serve in the future as a basis for a continuing dialogue among all concerned parties, they must be the result of a balanced approach. The right balance has to be established notably regarding two questions: the addressees and the actual contents of such standards.

The envisaged standards should be addressed to those who are able to create political and socio-economic tensions in the field of concern and to endanger a peaceful development process, i.e., they must contain principles for both TNEs [18] and host as well as home countries. Why? Because both TNEs and governments have the potential to create clashes and serious conflicts with considerable impact on international economic relations; and, in principle, both entities have the vigour to survive such confrontations, the state because of its plenitude of powers derived from its sovereign status, the TNE because of its transnational structure.

It is actually quite shortsighted if developing countries advocate that the standards should cover only the behaviour of TNEs. It is a matter of equity, credibility, and moral acceptability that these standards reflect the real political power relations and create "rights and obligations" for all parties concerned, in particular as it is possible that they will have to be accepted on a voluntary basis and that the international community will have to rely on their political and moral weight. This view is not, of course, based on the assumption that a formal reciprocity exists between governments and TNEs. There can be no dispute over the fact that these two entities are qualitatively different participants in international relations, [19] though during the last two decades there have been some interesting developments affecting the traditional notion of "subject of international law". [20] The standards, on the other hand, should also take into account that TNEs, due to their transnational structure, may enjoy particular business opportunities and possibly operate in areas which are not under national control.

In the same vein, the content of the standards has to reflect an equitable balance of the interest of all parties involved. There must be both principles which TNEs have to observe in their dealings with governments, groups, or individuals in the countries where they operate, and principles of governmental policies, i.e., host and home country policies. The latter might comprise, for instance, the obligation of home governments to refrain from using TNEs as an excuse to interfere in the internal affairs of other countries, and principles of host country policies, such as investment protection and national treatment, [21] as well as principles designed to reduce the potential of conflict built up by the use of governmental investment incentives and disincentives. [22] As a flanking measure there should also be a standard designed to ensure intergovernmental cooperation and exchange of information.

Starting from this working hypothesis, three basic categories of possible provisions may be contained in the envisaged set of standards: provisions addressed to TNEs and intended to influence their conduct; provisions addressed to states and dealing with the treatment of direct investment and TNEs; and finally, provisions addressed to states and dealing with intergovernmental cooperation. These three subject areas will be dealt with in the following three subsections.

On the basis of the considerations on the real and perceived impact of TNEs in Chapter Three, [23] a survey of existing guidelines and codes of conduct pertaining to direct investment and TNE activities, [24] notably the OECD Guidelines and an evaluation of the negotiations underway in the U.N. Commission on Transnational Corporations, [25] the following provisions to be contained in a world-wide set of standards for direct investment and TNE activities are thus identified:

2.2.4. *Principles for TNEs*

The standards should include the following principles for TNEs:

—respect of national sovereignty and observance of domestic laws, regulations, and administrative practices: the respect for national sovereignty would notably concern the exercise of sovereignty of the respective host countries over their resources and economic activities within their territories;

—adherence to economic goals and development objectives: consistent with the need to maintain the viability of their operations, TNEs should take measures to ensure that their activities are compatible with and make a positive contribution toward the achievement of the economic goals and established development objectives of the countries in which they operate;

—adherence to socio-cultural objectives and values: TNEs should be in touch with governments with a view to avoiding that their practices, products, or services cause distortions in basic cultural patterns or have socio-cultural effects considered undesirable by the countries concerned; this principle is based on the assumption that the ruling class in the respective countries identifies with and defends its own cultural heritage;

—respect for human rights and fundamental freedoms: this is a vital and delicate subject. The principle finds its application in particular in the field of employment practices. TNEs should not discriminate on the basis of race, colour, sex, religion, language, social origin, or political and other opinions. If Western market economies are prepared to fight in a convincing and consistent way for an economic system based on liberalism and freedom, they must propagate and implement vigourously such a principle. [26] The case of South Africa has shown, however, how delicate the implementation of this principle can be: the EEC countries have adopted a voluntary code of conduct for TNEs that supports equal pay and working conditions and the right of black workers to unionise, even though implementation of some of these provisions would violate South African law;

—non-interference in internal political affairs: TNEs should notably abstain from activities of a political nature which are inconsistent with domestic legislation or established practice in these countries;

—non-interference in intergovernmental relations: TNEs should not act as instruments for the advancement of foreign policy objectives of governments, unless they operate in accordance with intergovernmental cooperative arrangements; TNEs should also not request governments to act on their behalf in any manner that exceeds normal diplomatic representation;

—abstention from corrupt practices: both active bribery, i.e., the act of offering, promising, or giving a bribe to a "public official" by "any person" and passive bribery, i.e., the act of soliciting, demanding, or receiving a bribe by a "public official" should be considered criminal. The respective governments would have to apply the same principle to "those who demand". "Illicit payments" should be attacked vigorously. The U.S. have done so by adopting the Foreign Corrupt Practices Act of 1977. [27] This legislation reflects considerable foresight: even if it implies short-term disadvantages for certain enterprises, in the long run, it will help to ensure the survival of liberalism by renouncing the unacceptable face of capitalism and by enhancing the integrity and credibility of the liberal Western economic system;

—ownership and control: TNEs should notably ensure that the control shared by local partners as determined by equity or contractual terms in non-equity arrangements can be effectively exercised;

—balance of payments and financing: to the extent that the viability of their commercial activities is maintained, TNEs should contribute to the promotion to the greatest extent possible of the diversification of exports from the countries where they do business. TNEs should, to the greatest extent possible, also be responsive to justified requests by governments in host countries, particularly developing countries, concerning the phasing, over an acceptable, agreed-upon, period of time of repatriation of capital or remittances of accumulated profits, dividends or intra-corporate payments, when the size and timing of such transfers would aggravate serious balance-of-payments problems for the countries in which TNEs do business. In the same vein, TNEs should not defer or advance current intra-corporate payments in a manner that would increase currency instability. Finally, TNEs should refrain from imposing restrictions — contrary to established development objectives of the countries in which they operate and beyond generally-accepted commercial practice — on their entities regarding the transfer of goods, services or funds, which would adversely affect the balance-of-payments of such countries;

—new forms of investment: the standards might also contain a principle designed to encourage TNEs (and governments) to make use of particular non-equity arrangements such as franchising, licensing and management contracts, which would avoid the establishment of the traditional foreign-owned entities. Such forms of depackaging, based on contractual arrangements [28] might, to a certain extent, increase the flexibility of host countries and TNEs and, at the same time, reduce tensions by diminishing the visibility of TNE activities. In particular, such new forms of investment might allow the developing host country to determine more exactly the target area and the actual impact of the TNEs' commercial activities, and thus ensure that the TNE provides the desired contribution to the development process. On the other hand, developing countries should be realistic enough to understand that they cannot expect from such contractual arrangements that these give them, in all cases, more control over their economic destiny than equity-linked investments. TNEs, for example, can still control the flow of resources to the host country as well as the access to foreign markets. Nevertheless, one might assume that "contracting" and the various forms of "industrial cooperation," which, to some extent (depending upon the precise type of business to be done) proved to be successful in TNE relations with Eastern countries, [29] will be used more extensively for TNE activities in developing countries;

—taxation and transfer pricing: TNEs should, upon request of the taxation authorities of the countries in which they operate — subject to some safeguards — provide the information necessary to determine correctly the taxes to be assessed in connection with their operations, including relevant information concerning their operations in other countries. TNEs should also refrain from making use of the particular facilities available to them, such as transfer pricing, which does not conform to an arm's-length standard, for modifying, in ways contrary to national law, the tax base upon which members of the group are assessed;

—competition and restrictive business practices: TNEs should, in particular, refrain from actions which would adversely affect competition in the "relevant market" by abusing a dominant position of market power, for instance, refrain from anti-competitive acquisitions, predatory behaviour toward competitors, unreasonable refusals to deal, anti-competitive abuse of industrial property rights, discriminatory pricing, and using such pricing transactions between affiliated enterprises as a means of adversely affecting competition outside these enterprises. TNEs should refrain from restrictive agreements which adversely affect or eliminate competition; they should allow purchasers, distributors and licensees freedom to resell, export, purchase and develop their operations consistent with law and sound commercial practice. — Within UNCTAD multilaterally-agreed-upon principles for the control of restrictive business practices are under negotiation; the outcome of these negotiations will be of great importance. It might be recalled here that competition

and anti-trust rules stem from free market assumptions and have a powerful tendency to liberalise trade and competition and to make free market converts out of those who are authorised to "enforce" them;[30]
—transfer of technology: TNEs should endeavour to ensure that their activities fit satisfactorily into the scientific and technological policies and plans of the countries where they operate, and that they contribute to the development of national scientific and technological capacities, including the establishment and improvement in host countries of their capacity to innovate. TNEs should endeavour not to favour the "brain drain" from developing to developed countries. TNEs should notably do research into the particular technology that is most adaptable for use in the different developing countries where they do business. All this would, of course, require that developing countries elaborate a consistent national technology policy. It was expected that the UNCTAD V meeting in Manila in May 1979 would reach substantive agreement on a code of conduct regarding technology transfer. Agreement proved impossible, however, because the industrialized countries were not prepared to accept a legally-binding code. UNCTAD has now convened another round of negotiations. The U.N. Conference on Science and Technology for Development, held in Vienna in August 1979, has postponed the questions relating to TNEs. They will have to be dealt with by the U.N. General Assembly;
—employment and labour: TNEs should respect the right of their employees to be represented by trade unions and other bona fide organisations of employees and engage in constructive negotiations with a view to reaching agreement on employment conditions. TNEs should provide information to representatives of employees which would enable them to obtain a true view of the performance of the entity. TNEs should observe standards of employment and industrial relations not less favourable than those observed by comparable employers in the host country. TNEs should, to the greatest extent practicable, utilise, train, and prepare for upgrading members of the local labour force; TNEs should also train and employ local nationals in higher management functions; finally, it is vital that TNEs enable authorised representatives of their employees to conduct negoti-

ations on collective bargaining or labour management relations issues with representatives of management who are authorised to take decisions on the matters under negotiation. In the area of employment and labour there exist, in the meantime, standards with world-wide coverage containing a set of principles dealing with the social aspects of TNE activities particularly in developing countries;[31]

—consumer protection: TNEs should perform their business activities in a way which does not impose dangers to the health and safety of consumers; they should disclose to the public in the countries in which they operate all appropriate information regarding the contents and the possible hazardous effects of the products they produce or market;

—environmental protection: TNEs should endeavour to contribute to the protection of the environment and make efforts to develop and apply adequate technologies for this purpose;

—disclosure of information: TNEs should provide to the public in the countries in which they do business, at least annually, clear and comprehensible information designed to improve understanding of the structure, activities, and policies of the respective TNE as a whole. Such information should supplement information required by national laws, regulation and administrative practices, and be provided in a consolidated form. It should include financial as well as non-financial items, such as the structure of the transnational corporation, the main activities of its entities, the operating results and sales, significant new investment, the sources and uses of funds, the research and development expenditure, the policies followed in intragroup pricing and the accounting principles used in compiling and consolidating this information.

It should be made clear in this part of the envisaged standards that the principles for TNEs are not aimed at introducing differences of treatment between TNEs and domestic enterprises. Wherever relevant, they should reflect good practice for all.

2.2.5. *Principles for host and home countries*

The prospective standards for direct investment and TNE activities should include in addition the following principles for

governmental policies, legislation, and administrative practices:
—First, the basic principle of free entry and exit of foreign
capital and invisible transactions, allowing for exceptions and
varying degrees of liberalisation. As in the area of trade, the
basic approach to foreign direct investment should be a liberal
one; at least there should be a general understanding that such a
liberal concept should be accepted as a reference framework for
governmental behaviour. This liberal approach, which is not a
rigid, dogmatic and undifferentiated claim for liberalism as an
end in itself but a means to attempt an optimum allocation of
resources, should apply to both the traditional capital movements and the new forms of investment. Experience shows,
however, that countries will accept such a principle only if it
provides for safeguards, exceptions, and derogations, taking into
account the special constraints prevailing in developing countries and allowing for the necessary amount of screening designed to ensure that the effects of foreign direct investment
and TNE activities on the national economy do not conflict
with vital objectives in the field of economic, social, and, in
particular, developing policy. The survey in Chapter Four has
shown that, while there are, of course, varying degrees of governmental interference, certain countries attempt to control
direct investment and TNE activities to a considerable extent.
In many cases, such controls may be necessitated by a country's
fundamental economic and political intersts; in other cases, the
existing degree of governmental control and interference may,
in fact, not be justifiable by valid economic and political reasons. In the latter case, the existence of the proposed basic
principle of freedom of capital movements and invisible transactions — provided it has been accepted — might help to gener-
ate political pressure on certain countries to get rid of unjustifiable controls and restrictions. It should be underlined here
that the very objective of redeployment, which is so vital for
the industrialisation and advancement of the middle-income
group of developing countries requires a liberal framework and
economic and legal security.
—Second, creation of a positive investment climate by host
countries. This principle would imply the following: trans-

parency and clear definition of national policies, laws, regulations and administrative practices significantly affecting private foreign direct investment and TNE activities.

—Stability of the above policies, laws, regulations and administrative practices of governments. Necessary changes to be made in the light of evolving circumstances should take place in an orderly way with proper regard to the rights of investors established at the time: (*a*) Non-discrimination and national treatment[32] for foreign investors. (*b*) Timely and unrestricted transfer of the income from investment capital and repatriation of capital when the investment is terminated, unless exceptional measures are required by particular balance-of-payments difficulties. (*c*) Fair and equitable treatment of the investor's property. In cases where the host country deprives, directly or indirectly, a foreign investor of its property, just and effective compensation should be paid. Any such deprivation should be exclusively for a public purpose, non-discriminatory and in accordance with due process of law.[33] (*d*) Rapid solution of possible disputes between host countries and foreign investors and availability of access to arbitration. Arbitration procedures should be transparent and mutually satisfactory.

—Third, industrialised home countries should be ready to respond positively to requests from developing countries for technical assistance, notably concerning investment matters, and to seek ways of strengthening and developing the public and mixed financial institutions that can act as promoters of, associates in, and/or financiers for investment projects in developing countries.

—Fourth, home and host countries should cooperate in order to establish and make use of a multilateral investment insurance scheme, which might notably cover the following types of risks: expropriation, certain types of excessive governmental restrictions on conversion and transfer of capital, armed conflicts, or civil unrest — all this only in cases where insurance through commercial channels at reasonable terms cannot be obtained. To be eligible, investments should be of such a nature as to contribute significantly to the economic development of the host country. Membership should be as wide as possible, in-

cluding the developing countries as well as the traditional capital-exporting countries which already have national guarantee
schemes. The multilateral investment insurance scheme could be
administered by a multilateral investment guarantee corporation
or agency. [34] Such a scheme might hedge against the danger of
excessive political involvement between the capital-exporting
and -importing governments. It might also reduce undue competition among capital-exporting countries. It should include a
penalty for the country which expropriates without compensation and due process. Otherwise, the scheme might be considered an incentive for governmental restrictions and measures
with detrimental effects for foreign investors.

—Finally, recognition of the interests of other countries affected by official investment incentives and disincentives to international direct investment: as explained in Chapter Four,[35]
there exists a dangerous potential for international conflict due
to the increasing use of investment incentives. In particular,
there may now be growing concern in home countries about
possible unfavourable effects of foreign direct investment,
notably on domestic employment, the balance-of-payments and
tax revenues because of certain host country policies designed
to tilt the benefit of direct investment in their direction. The
latter might be considered by home countries as an artificial
diversion of the benefits of international direct investment
flows and trigger off international conflicts. There is a need for
world-wide international standards providing for a commitment
by participating countries to give due weight to the intersts of
other countries affected by specific laws, regulations and administrative practices intended to influence international investment decisions of TNEs. Such a commitment should furthermore provide that participating countries endeavour to make
such measures as transparent as possible so that their importance and purpose can be clearly ascertained and that information on them can be made readily available. In addition, the
respective standards might also provide for consultation and
possibly arbitration at the request of the country which considers that its interest (i.e., its flow of international direct invest-

ment) may be adversely affected by the impact of measures taken by another country. [36] In the application of this principle and in the respective consultations developed countries will have to take into account the particular situation of developing nations. Developing countries are often more vulnerable and may need more protection. Thus, developed countries have to waive, to some extent, their claim to the enforcement of the general legal principle of "mutuality" and must accept a "double standard" of economic rights and duties. The consultation procedures may help, later on in the development process, to remove such exceptions to the basic liberal principle which are not any more justifiable on economic grounds.

2.2.6. *Intergovernmental cooperation*

Host and home governments should agree to cooperate in order to make the envisaged standards for direct investment and TNE activities as effective as possible. This cooperation might create the necessary countervailing power and thus help to alleviate public concern about TNE activities. Governments should exchange information with regard to the above principles.

Some of the institutional aspects of this cooperation, in particular the participation of TNEs and other interested groups, such as the trade unions, will be further explored in the following section.

In the framework of this cooperation, governments could, inter alia, also resolve the difficulties stemming from conflicting legal requirements or jurisdictional claims and reduce unnecessary and counterproductive legal and administrative restrictions in order to allow direct investment and TNE activities to make the greatest possible contribution to development.

2.3. *Legal nature of the standards and institutional questions*

While there exists a broad consensus in the U.N. framework that a set of standards for direct investment and TNE activities may be desirable, the debate about whether such standards or codes of conduct should be binding or of a voluntary nature continues. Of course, those who doubt the wisdom or value of a set of standards and subscribe to the consensus only because of the existing political pressure, tend to support the position that such standards should be voluntary. But many who think that such standards are desirable also urge that they be voluntary rather than binding. An alternative position is that the legal nature of the standards should be determined only after their substantive provisions are agreed to, on the assumption that the more acceptable the substance, the more reasons there are to agree that the standards be binding. Throughout the negotiations on codes of conduct in the U.N., developed countries have argued that the codes should establish general equitable principles but should not be legally binding. [37] Developing countries, on the other hand, have called for codes of conduct that would contain specific rules and be legally binding for all parties concerned. [38]

Because of the intensity of disagreement, determination of the legal nature of the codes at present under negotiation within the United Nations [39] may be postponed. The UNCTAD Intergovernmental Group on Transfer of Technology, for example, has been instructed to draft a code "without prejudice to its legal nature". [40] The results of the UNCTAD V meeting which took place in Manila in May 1979, have shown, however, that it may prove impossible to draft a code without some resolution of the deadlock concerning the legal nature of the code.

As the issues relating to the legal nature of standards for direct investment and TNE activities lead immediately to the question of a possible implementation and enforcement machinery, some thought has also to be given to the institutional aspects of monitoring, surveillance, and possibly enforcement of the prospective standards.

2.3.1. *The legal nature: a law in evolution*

The debate on the legal nature of standards for direct investment and TNE activities is complicated by ambiguity and confusion concerning the consequences of accepting a "binding" or "voluntary" approach. A rational policy choice is, in particular, hampered by the misperception that binding and voluntary enforcement are opposites and the only choices, and that the effectiveness of the prospective standards depends upon their binding legal nature. In reality there is a spectrum of "enforcement" alternatives permitting a variety of approaches both initially and in the long run. [41] It should be recognised that the legal nature of the standards and the types of effectuating mechanisms employed to give effect to such standards may well vary according to the subject matter being covered and the degree of international consensus existing or obtainable with regard to that subject matter.

A single set of standards dealing with the whole range, substantive and procedural, of issues pertaining to international direct investment and the activities of TNEs may be practicable only on a so-called voluntary basis, [42] while the break-down of the set of standards into different instruments, each dealing with a particular subject may lead to a continuum of implementation alternatives. To illustrate this: a code dealing with international bribery may well be appropriate for a binding agreement (convention) providing for some sort of enforcement in the light of the comparatively high degree of international consensus condemning this practice. In the same vein, an instrument designed to achieve intergovernmental consultation, exchange of information, or dispute settlement concerning certain issues covered by the different instruments (for instance, the questions relating to the exceptions and derogations from the principle of free entry and exit of foreign capital and invisible transactions, the issues pertaining to investment incentives or disincentives, or other home and host country policies regarding direct investment and the activities of TNEs) may ideally also reflect an agreement of states. Codes dealing with restrictive business practices probably fall somewhere between the extremes, since this is a technical subject in which there is some history of international consensus in condemning certain practices, but there still exists great variation in the extent and approach of national laws on the subject. [43] Other provisions to be contained in the standards, for instance, some of those concerning good corporate citizenship, may be of a "voluntary" nature.

But what is the true meaning of "binding" and "voluntary",

and how would the various standards apply to the behaviour of private enterprises, given that they are not primary subjects of international law and normal parties to international agreements? While the traditional distinction between "subjects" and "objects" of international law has been blurred[44] (e.g., by the imposition of international responsibility on individuals for war crimes and by the establishment of tribunals before which individuals could accuse states of violations of human rights,[45] it would still not be legally possible for commercial enterprises to be signatories of international conventions or codes of conduct. In deciding, therefore, the extent to which such agreements and arrangements would create rights and obligations for TNEs, it has to be determined whether their conduct would be regulated by international institutions authorised to enforce the pertinent standards or by national legislation enacted pursuant to an international agreement; or, whether, on the other hand, the international agreement would provide merely that the principles for enterprises would be promulgated jointly by the governments to the TNEs operating in their territories.[46]

A "binding" instrument to be implemented on the basis of reciprocity[47] by national authorities might provide a good deal of legal security that should appeal to TNEs as well, provided the pertinent standards are equitable.

A "voluntary" instrument, on the other hand, need not be deprived of the force of the law. Once an international consensus on "voluntary" instruments is reached, the principles as agreed can have considerable moral and practical force on the conduct of both states and enterprises.[48] The understanding and expectation in reaching such an agreement or arrangement is that states will modify their practices to conform to the understandings of the "voluntary" agreement. Departure from such an agreement could subject a state and/or the concerned enterprise to pressure or "persuasion" from affected parties, which could be, under certain circumstances, a rather effective sanction: governments may, for instance, be brought under concerted political pressure if they do not recommend to "their" enterprises to follow the respective standards; or if they are not prepared to get rid of unjustifiable restrictions on the free entry and exit of capital and invisible transactions; or if they apply investment incentives having detrimental effects on the economies of other countries by distorting international investment flows. Non-complying TNEs may, on the other hand, be deprived of diplomatic protection or not obtain investment insurance or financing through national or international schemes.

Moreover, under certain conditions, it is possible that "voluntary" codes might pass into the general corpus of customary international law and thus become a source of law. Thus, voluntary instruments may, upon their general acceptance, become a source of law which must be applied.

As has been said already,[49] there are clear indications that the structure of international law is changing. The reshaping and development of the international economic law is part of the process leading to a new international economic system. In particular, the international legal system for direct investment and TNE activities which will be a major part of the future economic system, is, at present, still in a comparatively early stage of development, though there are varying degrees of evolution: those areas which already have a higher degree of specificity and multilateral acceptance may be covered by binding instruments, while other parts which are still very much in evolution and subject to continuous multilateral negotiation may be contained in "living instruments " which in present parlance are described as "voluntary". While binding instruments, of course, still are the ideal form of legal enactments, voluntary instruments may, as just explained, notwithstanding their constant evolution, significantly contribute to the security of law. The different instruments, even if not incorporated into the national law, may orient the behaviour of TNEs because the latter may wish to include the pertinent principles into their self-regulatory codes of conduct and general corporate standards.

The adoption of several instruments of varying binding force raises a number of problems. First, with respect to the time element: the negotiation and the coming into effect of legally binding instruments is likely to take longer than that of non-binding ones, due to the domestic processes of approval and ratification. In the case of a single set of standards which are partly legally binding and partly voluntary, a considerable time lag between the completion dates of the two parts would arise. Secondly, if some topics would seem to be left out of the instrument, its equilibrium, as perceived by participating governments, may suffer, making the balancing of positions and concessions among participating states more difficult.

The solution might be to elaborate a general balanced, non-binding framework along the lines of the principles set out above in section 2 of this chapter, on which basis further refinement could take place leading to a number of specific binding agreements.

While searching for solutions, it must, however, be clearly understood that developing countries are interested in advancing the development of the new international law as fast as possible and in having as many binding agreements as possible. They are convinced that mere guidelines would not satisfy their needs. Developing countries see temselves as relatively powerless against TNEs, both in negotiation with them and in enforcement of their national laws and regulations. Obtaining information about the practices of TNEs, for example, appears difficult for developing countries, when the headquarters and major offices of the enterprises are elsewhere. [50] Thus, they envisage a strong enforcement role for the home countries of TNEs operating within the developing host countries. Developing countries argue that only a multilaterally-binding code containing penalties for non-observance will enjoin TNEs, whose contribution is vital for the development process, from simply abandoning the countries that attempt to regulate them and relocating in a country that takes a more benign view of the respective TNE's practices.

On the other hand, this sort of binding instrument, in which the home country has to guarantee the good behaviour of "its" enterprises would, in many instances lead to the exercise of extra-territorial jurisdiction and possibly to excessive home country involvement in the internal affairs of host countries, thus creating new sources of international conflict.

The potential for international conflict might, however, become less important if countries would succeed in developing adequate mechanisms for intergovernmental cooperation.

2.3.2. *Institutional aspects*

Pope John's encyclical *"pacem in Terris"*, which has given a new, unprecedented impulse to the search for peace and world order, states that "... the public authority of the world community must tackle and solve problems of an economic, social, political, or cultural character which are posed by the universal common good. For, because of the vastness, complexity, and urgency of those problems, the public authorities of the individual states are not in a position to tackle them with any hope of resolving them satisfactorily."

Many proposals exist for improving the United Nations system. [51] Most of them have limited their attention to the elimination of war. But war is not something that can be added to or removed from the total fabric of the social, political, and economic lives of people. Today's major challenges are not only of a military but also of an economic and socio-political nature, as evidenced by the prominence of the problems relating to the new economic system. Under these circumstances, the maintenance of world military security is too narrow an objective for a world-wide international organisation like the U.N. A U.N. Security Council should therefore deal not only with military but also with economic security.[52] Later on this task might be assumed by a "world development board" or "authority", the establishment of which has been discussed above.[53]

This would not mean, however, that together with the improvement of the U.N. system and the reorientation and enlargement of its tasks and responsibilities, a system of worldwide central industrial planning and *dirigiste* interference involving complicated and costly administrative machinery should be introduced. Quite the opposite, the reorientation of the U.N. system must help to establish a framework, a new international economic system, which would safeguard the vital force of economic liberalism and allow it to make an optimum contribution to development.

Thus, the idea of creating a "world production authority" and charging it with the control and general management of certain transnational enterprises is not acceptable, as this would be the beginning of world-wide state capitalism, a system which is not suitable for the conduct of international economic relations. Even the centrally planned Eastern countries would not accept that "their" TNEs be controlled by an international production authority. The entrepreneurial freedom and the creativity of TNEs must be preserved. The highest executives of TNEs and the world statesmen may act as countervailing forces and partners but their functions should not be intermingled.

However, as in the framework of a liberal national economy, there is also in the world economic system a need for social corrections and mechanisms designed to reduce the potential for conflict.

If there are disputes on the implementation of the prospective standards for direct investment and TNEs, countries may — depending upon the specific nature of the complaint and the precise legal basis — address themselves to the International Court of Justice. But TNEs could not be heard by this international forum as the Statute of the International Court of Justice does not empower it to hear cases in which individuals or legal persons are parties. [54] Countries might, therefore, consider the establishment of a special administrative or judicial agency to ensure the harmonious application of the standards by all parties. But neither the developing nor the developed countries have proposed that such entities be created. For the developing countries this position may stem from their glorification of nationalism and their fear and rejection of laws or law enforcement lying outside national control.

Thus, at present, the appropriate solution might be to provide for exchange of information and to establish consultation procedures, i.e., to agree on an obligation to consult within a multilateral framework, e.g., the U.N. Commission for Transnational Corporations, when a party requests these multilateral consultations; prior informal consultations would of course, not be precluded by such a procedure. Such multilateral consultations and review sessions may bring countries or TNEs which do not abide by the standards under concerted political pressure; at the same time, they might induce certain countries to get rid of unjustifiable restrictions on foreign investment flows and to avoid resorting to measures by which they could try to solve their own economic problems at the expense of other countries with damaging consequences in the economic, social, and political fields.

If the dispute cannot be settled on the basis of the consultation, the concerned parties could have recourse to international arbitration. The arbitrators would be guided by the standards as a primary or supplementary source of law. Such an approach would have the advantage of representing a compromise on both sides. Developing countries, particularly those in Latin America, would be compromising by accepting arbitration rather than staying with their usual position under the Calvo doctrine. [55] The developed countries would be compromising by conceding that the standards — even the "voluntary" parts of them — would have the force of law within the context of agreed binding arbitration.

Arbitration may, however, be inappropriate or inapplicable in many situations which may arise under the standards. [56] Thus, if the dispute cannot be settled on the basis of obligatory consultation, there might be a procedure of "mandatory international conciliation" authorising the establishment of an International Panel of Conciliators; this form of conciliation has been accepted in the Convention on a Code of Conduct for Liner Conferences. [57] As is generally the case with conciliation, parties to the dispute need not accept the recommendation of the conciliators, but there is, nonetheless, a certain pressure to impel the parties toward agreement.

Enterprises, trade unions, and other concerned groups should have, in general, a right to participate in these procedures to the extent that their interests are affected. TNEs should have a right to request consultation in those cases where home or host countries are in violation of provisions addressed to them and dealing with the treatment of TNEs.

In addition, countries, enterprises and trade unions, and other interested groups should have the right to ask, as necessary, for interpretation of the standards by the forum where the multilateral consultations take place.

The results of the consultation, arbitration, or conciliation procedures and of interpretation of the standards should be made public. This provision may, in fact, be a rather effective sanction for those who violate the standards. In addition, publication is necessary for creating "case law" and norm refinement with the result of increasing legal security.

Experience shows that most nations prefer to use non-public, bilateral diplomatic approaches rather than formalised procedures. Agreement to consultation procedures may be seen as a cosmetic formula for indicating a cooperative attitude and disguising unwillingness to surrender parts of national sovereignty by creating powerful international institutions. On the other hand, agreement to consultation — notably obligatory consultation — about adherence to rules and standards inevitably implies a greater dedication to abiding by and obeying those standards than would be the case if the agreement to consult had not been reached.

Notes to chapter seven

1. See The Conference Board, *Multinationals in Contention*, New York, 1978, p. 229.

2. In many instances, however, quite important changes have taken place on the bilateral level; see Chapter Four, section 2.2.3.

3. This appreciation is based on a review of the work of the Fourth Session of the U.N. Commission of Transnational Enterprises from 16-26 May 1978 in Vienna; see the pertinent summaries and the documents cited in *The CTC Reporter*, no. 5, September 1978.

4. See Chapter Six, section 1.2.1.

5. See OECD, *International Investment and Multinational Enterprises*, 1976; also OECD, "International Investment and Multinational Enterprises," *Review of the 1976 Declaration and Decisions*, 1979; and, Grewlich, *Direct Investment in the OECD Countries*, 1978.

6. See Chapter Four, section 2.1.

7. See Chapter Three, section 3.

8. In this context, see Sen S.C., *Multinational Corporations in the Developing Countries*, Calcutta, 1978.

9. See Chapter Three, section 3.

10. See Chapter One, section 6 and Chapter Six, section 2.3.

11. See *Black's Law Dictionary*, 4th ed., 1968, p. 323.

12. This idea is also advanced by Garelli, *Vers un code de conduite international à l'intention des sociétés transnationales*, 1977, p. 185.

13. See Chapter One, section 4.

14. See Chapter Four, section 4.

15. See the review of national policies in Chapter Four.

16. See Hellmann, *Transnational Control of Multinational Corporations*, 1977.

17. See Chapter Five, sections 1 and 3.

18. An attempt to clarify the notion of "TNE" has been made in Chapter Two, section 2.2.

19. See Chapter One, section 6.

20. See Mosler, *Die Erweiterung des Kreises der Völkerrechtssubjekte*, in Zeitschrift für ausländisches öffentliches Recht und Völkerrecht 22, p. 1 (1962).

21. "National treatment" means that governments are not allowed to discriminate against enterprises under foreign control in relation to domestic enterprises; cf. Grewlich, *Direct Investment in the OECD Countries*, op. cit., p. 95.

22. See Chapter Four, section 4.

23. See Chapter Three, section 3.

24. See Chapter Five, sections 1, 2 and 3; titles IV and V of the recently finalized convention between the EEC and the ACP countries (Lomé II) were also taken into consideration.

25. See U.N., *Transnational Corporations: Code of Conduct, Formulations by the Chairman*, E/C AC.2/8 (1978), (reproduced in *CTC Reporter*, no. 6, p. 5. (1979)).

26. EEC countries have therefore made an attempt to include the principle of respect for human rights into the Lomé II agreement.

27. Public Law 95-123 of 19 December 1977.

28. See Chapter Three, section 1.5.

29. See Chapter Four, section 2.1.

30. See Davidow and Chiles, *The U.S. and the Issue of the Binding or Voluntary Nature of International Codes of Conduct Regarding Restrictive Business Practices*, American Journal of International Law, vol. 72. p. 247 (271) (1978).

31. ILO, *Tripartite Declaration of Principles Concerning Multinational Enterprises and Social Policies*, 1977.

32. See note 21 in this chapter.

33. See the legal considerations in Chapter Six, sections 2.1.3. and 2.1.4.

34. The International Bank for Reconstruction and Development (World Bank) has been working on such a scheme.

35. See Chapter Four, section 4.

36. See OECD, *International Investment and Multinational Enterprises*, 1976; OECD is going to strengthen its efforts in this area, cf. *OECD Observer* 99, p. 39 (1979); the World Bank has recently started work along similar lines.

37. Developed countries normally point to the voluntary nature of the OECD Guidelines. The European Parliament, however, has called for legally binding codes for TNE activities, but EC-commission lawyers anticipate that the rules may be binding for intra-community application but voluntary in relationships with other countries; see *Common Market Reports*, no. 433, pt. 1, at 1, 2 (1977).

38. This view is not supported by the Socialist countries of Eastern Europe, which, in many instances, join the most radical groups of developing countries in order to increase political pressure upon Western market economies. This shows that the Eastern countries prefer to keep their TNE activities as flexible as possible.

39. See Chapter Five, section 3.2.

40. See, e.g., U.N. Doc. TD/AC.1/4, at 2 (1976).

41. An attempt to clarify this question has been made in U.N. Commission on Transnational Corporations, *Transnational Corporations: Certain Modalities for Implementation of a Code of Conduct in Relation to its Possible Legal Nature*, E/D.10/AC.2/9 (December 1978); see also Davidow and Chiles, op. cit.

42. The notion of "voluntary" will be qualified later on.

43. See Davidow and Chiles, op. cit., p. 250.

44. See note 20.

45. As in the case of the European Convention for the Protection of Human Rights.

46. This approach has been taken in the OECD Guidelines.

47. It being understood that there must be agreed exceptions (preferential treatment) taking into account the particular needs and problems of developing countries. The principle of reciprocity should, on the other hand, ensure that it is not left to each government to decide the precise manner of incorporation into domestic law, with the result that uniformity of treatment would be jeopardized and that TNEs would be able to select the most favourable régime for their operations.

48. See Schachter, *The Twilight Existence of Non-binding International Agreements*, in American Journal of International Law, 71, p. 296 (1977).

49. Chapter Six, section 2.1.3.

50. It is for that reason that developing countries are strongly in favour of the elaboration of a comprehensive information system by the U.N. Centre on Transnational Corporations. Western industrialized countries are not entirely opposed to such a system but ask for adequate mechanisms of verification and control of the objectivity of information

which is being collected and for the inclusion of state-owned enterprises into the system.

51.   See e.g. *The Fund for the Republic, A Constitution for the World,* 1965.

52.   See Chapter One, section 4.

53.   See Chapter Six, section 2.2.9.

54.   Article 34, para 1 of the Statute of the International Court of Justice provides that "only states may be parties in cases before the Court".

55.   See note 31 in Chapter Four.

56.   See Davidow and Chiles, op. cit., p. 265.

57.   See Grewlich, *Die UN-Konvention über einen Verhaltenskodex für Linienkonferenzen* (The U.N. Convention on a Code of Conduct for Liner Conferences), Zeitschrift für ausländisches öffentliches Recht und Völkerrecht, vol. 35, p. 742 (1975).

Chapter Eight

CONCLUDING REMARKS

1. There is a vital need for world economic development. No country can stand on its own, and even the strongest ignore others at their own peril. This development requires a system of international relations, regional and global trade, international investment, transfer of know-how and communication in the political and economic field.

Development of the poor countries is not only in their interest; for the industrialised countries it is a moral duty to help them, but it also makes convincing economic and political sense, except for the shortsighted. Governments have to create a rational framework, unilaterally, bilaterally and multilaterally — but the entrepreneurial initiative has an enormous role to play.

Development aid is indispensable. But, the basic-needs approach is not enough. It is inevitable and natural that business moves abroad.

2. Developing countries still depend heavily on industrialised nations for new industrial processes and techniques. The overwhelming majority of these originate in developed countries, including the industrialized centrally-planned economies, which together are estimated to account for over 95 per cent of world spending in research and development. New technology is transferred to developing nations, notably to the middle-income developing countries, by diverse channels, including the capital goods imported by these countries and, in particular, direct investment by foreign TNEs. Countries at early stages of industrialisation tend to rely more heavily on transfer mechanisms such as foreign private investment that combine technology,

capital skills, marketing, and management in one package, while nations with more developed industrial structures are in a better position to define and contract for specific technology needs. Such arrangements do not, however, necessarily give them more control over their economic destiny than equity-linked investments, as TNEs still control the flow of resources to the host country as well as access to foreign markets. Moreover, the trend towards the various forms of "depackaging" and contracting is much slower in high technology industries, such as motor vehicles, petrochemicals, precision machine tools, and computers, where the sources of supply are limited and developing country buyers lack the requisite expertise.

3. Complaints about TNEs do exist and developing country leaders in particular suspect that certain TNEs do not always behave in one country as they do elswhere, where laws and regulations may be more adequately enforced. It is also alleged that the economic contribution of TNEs to development and prosperity could be much greater, because, according to host country leaders, TNEs fail to understand fully host country needs and aspirations. Because of such dissatisfaction, TNEs are increasingly exposed to a tightening web of regulations and controls — often contradictory — at both national and international levels, by which host, but also home countries seek to maximise benefits gained from TNE operations and to minimise disadvantages. In the future, the home country may even become the greatest challenge to transnational flexibility, as changing conditions and interest group pressures within developed home nations may force home governments to react to perceived disadvantages originating from the operations of "their own" TNEs. Thus, a potential for conflict exists which requires adequate surveillance and machinery for consultation and dispute settlement.

4. What transpires is an increasing confrontation between those trying to preserve the status quo and those who want to change it. We can observe a determined effort on the part of those who have yet to participate fully in the international economic sys-

tem to gain immediate and full access to the system and an equal right to all of its benefits. Thus, TNEs which are increasingly seen as permanent, integral elements in the international economic system and as symbols of its alleged injustice can expect to remain the source of contention for some time to come in the international arena.

On the other hand, there may be many governments which actually prefer the muddled situation that now exists in the negotiations on international investment and TNE activities, because many are afraid to cut off the benefits derived from TNEs by a too-quick resolution of the issues at stake. In addition, no group is willing to settle for less if it believes that later on it could have more.

5. Experience with international negotiations and multilateral economic diplomacy shows that the potential of conflict and harmful confrontation increases tremendously if negotiations come to a deadlock. Multilateral diplomats avoid this danger by arranging for an endless series of international conference where the focus of the North-South dialogue shifts from the U.N. General Assembly to UNCTAD, after that to a conference like the Conference on International Economic Cooperation (Paris), and following this, to a newly established U.N. forum which is called the "Plenary" (or "Overview") Committee and from there again to UNCTAD, after which it goes back to the U.N. General Assembly, and so on. The negotiations underway in the various fora of the U.N. system specialising in particular fields of international relations, such as the ECOSOC Commission on Transnational Corporations, are, to a large extent, conditioned by the events taking place in the varying centres of the North-South dialogue. This proves the political nature of all these negotiations. Progress is very slow and the danger of a global deadlock leading to radical confrontation, though unlikely at present, increases continuously.

In view of the millions of starving and suffering people, the danger for world peace and economic development and the short time available for solving the global problems confronting the world today, the present tactical game in multilateral diplomacy is not acceptable. Political leaders must resist the temptation to use meetings and conferences merely as a tactical device to play for time. Someone has to take the initiative to shift the international mood effectively from one of petty bargaining to one of an earnest search for synergies and convergencies in order to achieve a deep and unavoidable change in world relations.

The author defends the position that the Western market economies do have a moral duty and also a great direct interest to develop in cooperation with the South a global strategy in order to be responsive to the fundamental demands of the developing world. Because of the West's still formidable wealth of knowledge, experience, and intellectual and material resources, it should now make clear the responsibilities which Western democracies will have to bear in the process toward a new international economic system. It was the West which designed and dominated the "old" international system. It is, therefore, primarily the Western democracies' responsibility — and this is not a question of guilt but of moral duty — to assert their leadership to take up the planetary challenge for change, and to rethink and to reshape, together with the South, the bases of the international political, economic, and social system. No doubt, the necessary adaption will only be the result of a deep and long process, but this process cannot be allowed to be too lengthy either. This is not to say, of course, that the West alone should bear the economic and financial burden of the adjustment process. Other regions will have to join, notably the Eastern countries; the OPEC countries which create great difficulties to many developing countries by their oil price policy must further strengthen their development efforts.

6. The study has set out the major elements of a prospective international economic system. The proposed system is responsive to the particular needs of developing countries, while preserving the vital force of economic liberalism and the essential virtues of a free enterprise system. Without these virtues productivity would decline with detrimental consequences for the North and even worse for the South.

There exist varying degrees of economic planning in the national economies of developing countries. While at a certain stage of development, a sound degree of planning is often the appropriate way to overcome certain obstacles in a developing economy, it would be detrimental for the international economic system to accept a transposition of the economic systems of the centrally planned economies of the East and the South into the field of international economic relations. In addition to adjusting the international economic system to a more equitable allocation of resources and a just distribution of welfare, it must be a main objective of intergovernmental surveillance and monitoring in the field on international economic relations to guarantee the basically liberal character of the system. Western industrialised economies should lead the way and, for instance, reduce as far as possible protectionist practices which they have recently adopted. This is a difficult task in a period of slow growth and rising unemployment.

Economic liberalism is not a quasi-ideological aim in itself. The new international economic system will have to provide for, to the benefit of developing countries, varying numbers of temporary exceptions to the free play of market forces and for certain types of governmental initiatives, notably in the fields of trade and international investment. This would mean that, regarding the economic rights and duties of countries participating in the new international economic system, a "double standard" would be introduced, putting certain groups of developing countries on a temporary basis — i.e., as long as economically justifiable — into a priviledged position. Thus, certain developing countries would receive preferential treatment, certain concessions or particular advantages (for instance, the right to enjoy a certain amount of protection in the field of trade; the right to regulate the entry and exit of international investment flows by "screening", i.e., by investment incentives and disincentives and other measures of control and regulation; the right to adopt certain derogations from the principle of national treatment, etc.). It will be necessary to establish multilateral surveillance procedures to ensure that such exceptions from the basic liberal orientation of the new international economic system are granted only to those countries which are, because of the development process, particularly vulnerable and not able to stand the full pressure of the international economic system. To that extent, developed countries will have to waive their claim to the application of the legal principle of "mutuality". This is the "price" which the developed market economies will have to pay for the developing countries' adherence to a basically still liberal economic system.

Energy is an important aspect of the North-South dialogue and increasingly also of the "South-South dialogue" taking place between OPEC countries and less developed countries. If the Western countries welcome the inclusion of energy matters in the multilateral negotiations within the U.N. framework or in other fora, it should be understood that this is not a question of Western selfishness. In practice, all the actors on the world energy stage, the industrialised consuming countries, the oil-TNEs, the OPEC countries, the East European countries and, in particular, also the non-oil developing countries, have a strong interest in the stability and orderly development of the world energy market. Energy remains fraught with the highest political and even strategic significance, and there is always the potential danger that shortsighted policies from any quarter will lead to an aggressive and destructive scramble for scarce world energy supplies. In such a process, the non-oil developing countries, already extremely hard-hit by high energy costs, would suffer most.

It is indeed vital to be perfectly aware of the economic stress which the recent development of the world energy market put upon developing countries. They have observed the enormous economic upswing wich industrialised countries have experienced between 1950 and 1970. This expansion was, to a large extent, based on cheap oil. Oil was the engine of the Western economies. Oil has a crucial importance for developing countries. It stands for economic growth and wealth. It was expected that oil would play a major part in development plans; the number of oil-fired power stations which have been recently established in developing countries is evidence of this. The explosion of the oil price has now made many development plans non-operational in monetary terms. Under these circumstances, industrialised countries, which have the technological potential, have a moral obligation to help developing countries to diversify their energy resources and to develop alternative energy sources such as geothermal and, notably, solar energy. There is thus a great need for new forms of energy investments and for an appropriate transfer of technology. In this process of a worldwide restructuring of energy resources on the basis of new technologies the TNEs may have to play a decisive role, if the governments of developed and developing countries are able to induce the TNEs to assume new responsibilities. This applies in particular to the transnational oil companies, which are already strengthening their efforts in the field of energy diversification.

7. The process leading towards a new international economic system will not be an easy one. There may be years of bitter conflict ahead. During this process it is in the interest of TNEs and governments to avoid major clashes in the field of international investment. Every possible effort should, therefore, be made to bring as much security as possible into the international economic system.

One way of creating more political and economic security, to the extent that it is achievable in a period of rapid change, is to set out the "rules of the game", i.e., in the specific case of international investment to agree on a framework of standards for direct investment and TNE operations.

There exist different national approaches to the issues pertaining to international investment and TNE activities. As the issues are, however, of a global nature, there is a need for a world-wide approach comprising equitable standards for the behaviour of governments and TNEs which would create the necessary amount of confidence and security in international economic relations.

There have been and there still are numerous attempts to create such standards or codes of good conduct both on a self-regulatory basis (the business community) or as a result of governmental efforts on the national, regional, inter- and supranational level. In addition, trade unions and different pressure groups have also established similar guidelines. All these codes, guidelines, and instruments reflect different perceptions and interests. They show varying degrees of specificity and "compulsion". Two fundamental approaches may be distinguished: those which try to achieve a certain amount of policy coordination and the improvement of the international investment climate; and, those which are designed to alter the bargaining power. The latter approach is pursued by developing countries in the framework of the U.N.

This study has dealt with existing national and international approaches and on this basis with the underlying philosophy and the policy objectives of a prospective world-wide framework of standards. An outline of the provisions to be contained in the framework envisaged was set out. Particular attention has been given to the scope of addressees, to the legal nature of the standards, and to a number of institutional questions.

—The prospective world-wide standards for direct investment and TNE activities must be balanced with regard to the addressees and the contents. The standards would therefore comprise provisions addressed to TNEs and intended to influence their conduct in host and home countries (good corporate citizenship); provision addressed to states and dealing with the treatment of direct investment and TNEs (e.g., national treatment); and provisions addressed to states and dealing with intergovernmental cooperation (e.g., exchange of information, consultation, conciliation, or arbitration).

—The standards might include separate instruments of varying binding force. While the whole legal system of international direct investment and TNE activities is very much in evolution, those parts of the standards which are called "voluntary" should be seen as "living instruments", i.e., they are particularly subject to continuous negotiation in the framework of the process leading to a new international economic system. The "voluntary nature" does not, on the other hand, necessarily reduce the effectiveness of the respective instruments. The adoption of several instruments of varying binding force raises the problem of the equilibrium in the process of negotiations. It would thus be appropriate to adopt first a general, non-binding framework, on which basis further refinement could take place, leading to a number of more specific binding agreements.

—The standards must be kept under constant intergovernmental surveillance. There is a need for some institutional machinery providing for a forum of discussion among states and TNEs on matters related to the standards, in particular their application and the experience gained in their implementation. Procedures for exchange of information, obligatory consultation, conciliation or arbitration, and interpretation upon request must be established. TNEs and, to some extent, other interested groups, notably trade unions, have a right to participate in these procedures. The outcome of the procedures should be made public.

—Regarding the political substance of the proposed standards, they clearly intend to be responsive to the particular needs of developing countries and renounce the unacceptable face of capitalism, while preserving the vital force of economic liberalism and entrepreneurial freedom.

It is the purpose of the standards to establish the right balance between complete uncertainty and an overly-rigid legalistic approach, between freedom and responsibility, between liberalism and protection of the weaker party, between the uncontrolled use of sovereign rights and the exercise of transnational power.

The adoption of the world-wide framework of standards proposed in this study would preserve entrepreneurial creativity and corporate innovation capacity and, at the same time, ensure that TNEs make an effective contribution to world development and play a positive role in a new international system.

BIBLIOGRAPHY

Andrews, Kenneth, *The Concept of Corporate Strategy*, Homewood, Ill. 1971.

Ball, George W., "Cosmocorp: The Importance of Being Stateless," in Courtney C. Brown (ed.), *World Business*, New York 1970, p. 337.

Global Companies: The Political Economy of World Business. Englewood Cliffs 1975.

Bauer, P.T. and B.S. Yamey, *Against the New York Economic Order, Commentary*, April 1977, pp. 25-31.

Bergsten, Fred C., "Coming Investment Wars?," *Foreign Affairs*, vol. 53 (1974), pp. 135-152.

The Future of the International Economic Order: An Agenda for Research, Lexington, Mass. 1973.

Bertin, G.Y. and J.P. Escaffre, *Internationalisation des grandes banques mondiales*, Paris 1975.

Black's Law Dictionary, Revised 4th ed., St. Paul 1968.

Böckstiegel, K.H., *Die allgemeinen Grundsätze des Völkerrechts über Eigentumsentziehung*, Frankfurt 1963.

Boddewyn, Jean J., "Western European Policies Toward U.S. Investors," *The Bulletin* (New York University Graduate School of Business Administration, Institute of Finance), March 1974.

"Brandt-Commission". Independent Commission on International Development Issues, North-South: A programme for survival, 1980.

Business International Corporation, *Investing, Licensing and Trading Conditions Abroad*, New York 1976.

Operating in Latin America's Integrating Markets: ANCOM/ CACM/CAPRICOM/LAFTA, New York 1977.

Cairncross, Sir Alec, *Control of Longterm International Capital Movements*, Washington D.C. 1973.

Calvo, Carlos, *Le droit international théorique et pratique*, 5th ed., Paris 1896.

Camps, Miriam, *The Management of Interdependence*, Council of Foreign Relations, Washington 1974.

Club of Rome, *RIO-Reshaping the International Order* (Jan Tinbergen, Co-ordinator), New York 1976.

Commission of the European Economic Communities, "Multi-national Undertakings and Community Regulations, Communication from the Commission to the Council presented on 8 November 1973," *Bulletin of the European Communities*, Supplement 17/1973, Brussels 1973.

"Statute for European Companies — Amended Proposals for a Regulation," *Bulletin of the European Communities*, Supplement 4/1975, Brussels 1975.

Survey of Multinational Enterprises, vol. 1, Brussels 1976.

Curhan, J.P., W.H. Davidson and R. Suri, *Tracing the Multinationals*, Cambridge, Mass. 1977.

Davidow, Joel and Lisa Chiles, *The United States and the Issue of the Binding or Voluntary Nature of International Codes of Conduct regarding Restrictive Business Practices*, American Journal of International Law, vol. 72, p. 247 (1978).

Delupis, Ingrid, *Finance and Protection of Investments in Developing Countries*, Epping-Essex 1973.

Department of Trade and Industry (U.K.), *The impact of Foreign Direct Investment on the United Kingdom*, London 1973.

Diebold Institute, "Private Enterprises in a Post-Industrial Society," no. 2, *Business and Developing Countries*, New York 1973.

Donges, Juergen, "Zur Industrialisierungsprojektion der UNIDO, Bundesministerium für wirtschaftliche Zusammenarbeit," *Entwicklungspolitik*, Materialien no. 52, Bonn 1975.

Dunning, John H. (ed.), *The Multinational Enterprise*, London 1971.

Elmandjra, Mahdi, "Political Facets of the North-South Dialogue," *Forum for Correspondence and Contact*, vol. 10 (1978), p. 171.

European Parliament, "The Principles to be Observed by Enterprises and Governments in International Economic Activity (Lange/Gibbons Code)," *Parliament Working Documents*, no. 547/76 (1977).

European Trade Union Confederation (ETUC), "Demands of the European Trade Union Confederation for Company-Law Regulations for Multinational Enterprises," Executive Committee Paper, Brussels 1975.

Farer, Tom, "The United States and the Third World: A Basis for Accommodation," *Foreign Affairs*, vol. 54 (1975), pp. 79-97.

Fels, Gerhard, "The Choice of Industry Mix in the Division of Labour between Developed and Developing Countries," *Welwirtschaftliches Archiv*, vol. 108 (1972), pp. 71-99.

Fels, Gerhard, Klaus-Werner Schatz and Frank Wolter, "Der Zusammenhang zwischen Produktionsstruktur und Entwicklungsniveau," *Weltwirtschaftliches Archiv*, vol. 106 II (1971), p. 240.

Feuer, Guy, *Reflexions sur la Charte des Droit et Devoirs Economiques des Etats*, Revue Générale de Droit International Public, vol. 79 (1975), pp. 274-320.

Fischer, Fritz, "Die unabhängige Kommission für internationale Entwicklungsfragen ('Brandt-Commission')," *Europa-Archiv*, vol. 21 (1979), pp. 703-710.

Fischer, Per, "Technologie als Vehikel der Entwicklung", *Europa-Archiv* 1979, pp. 633-642.

Forrester, Jay W., "Counterintuitive Behaviour of Social Systems," *Technology Review*, Jan. 1971.

Friedman, Milton, *Capitalism and Freedom*, Chicago 1962.

Friedmann, W.G., *The Changing Structure of International Law*, New York 1964.

Galbraith, J.K., *The New Industrial State*, Boston 1967.

Garbe, Ottfried, "Friedrich List and His Relevance for Development Policy," *Intereconomics* (1977), pp. 251-256.

Garelli, Stephane, *Vers un code de conduite international à l'intention des sociétés transnationales*, Zürich 1977.

Girvan, N., "Corporate Imperialism: Conflict and Expropriation," *Transnational Corporations and Economic Nationalism in the Third World*, New York 1976.

Goetschin, Pierre, "L'entreprise multinationale, présent et futur," *Revue économique et sociale*, 31ème année, no. 1 (1973), pp. 7-20.

Government of Canada, *Foreign Direct Investment in Canada*, Ottawa 1972.

Grapin, Jacqueline, "Un échange de bons procédés," *Le Monde*, Paris 29 juin 1976.

Grewlich, Klaus, *Bedeutung und Funktionsweise des OECD-Kodex zur Liberalisierung des Kapitalverkehrs*, Recht der Internationalen Wirtschaft (1977), pp. 252-258.

Die UN-Konvention für Linienkonferenzen, Zeitschrift für ausländisches öffentliches Recht und Völkerrecht, vol. 35 (1975), pp. 742-758.

Direct Investment in the OECD Countries, Alphen aan den Rijn 1978.

Grubel, Herbert J., "The Case against the New International Economic Order," *Weltwirtschaftliches Archiv*, vol. 113 (1977), pp. 284-307.

Gutman, P. and R. Arkwright, "Coopération industrielle tripartite Est-Ouest-Sud: Evaluation financière et analyse des modalités de paiement et de financement," *Politique Etrangère*, vol. 41 no. 6 (1976), pp. 615-641.

Hellman, Rainer, *Transnational Control of Multinational Corporations*, New York 1977.

Hymer, S. and R. Rowthorn, "Multinational Corporations and International Oligopoly: The Non-American Challenge," in Kindleberger (ed.), *The International Corporations*, Boston 1970.

Iffland, Charles and Antoine Galland, *Les Investissments Industriels Suisses au Mexique*, Lausanne 1978.

International Centre for the Settlement of Investment Disputes, *11th Annual Report 1976/77*, Washington D.C. 1977.

Convention on the Settlement of Investment Disputes between States and Nationals of Other States, Wahington 1966.

"Investment Laws of the World" (looseleaf).

International Chamber of Commerce, *Bilateral Treaties for International Investment,* Paris 1977.

> *Guidelines for International Investment,* 2nd ed., Paris 1974.

> *Recommendations to Combat Extortion and Bribery in Business Transactions,* Paris 1977.

International Confederation of Free Trade Unions, *Charter on Multinational Enterprises,* Mexico 1975.

International Labour Organisation, *Tripartite Declaration of Principles Concerning Multinational Enterprises and Social Policy,* Geneva 1977.

International Monetary Fund, *Balance of Payments Manual,* 3rd ed., Washington D.C. 1966.

Ipsen, Hans-Peter, *Europäisches Gemeinschaftsrecht,* Tübingen 1972.

Jacoby, Neil, *Corporate Power and Social Responsibility,* New York 1973.

Jacot, S.-P., "L'européanisation des entreprises," *Revue économique et sociale,* vol. 36 (1978), pp. 82-87.

Johnson, Arthur, *Government Business Relations,* Columbus, Ohio 1965.

Juhl, Paul Georg, "Prospects for Foreign Direct Investment in Developing Countries," in Giersch (ed.), *Reshaping the World Economic Order,* Tübingen 1976, pp. 173-207.

Jungnickel, Rolf, "Die Wettbewerbsposition der deutschen multinationalen Unternehmen im internationalen Vergleich" in Däubler Wolfgang and Karl Wohlmut (ed.), *Transnationale Konzerne und Weltwirtschaftsordnung,* Baden-Baden 1977.

Keynes, John Maynard, *The General Theory of Employment, Interest and Money,* London 1936.

Kindleberger, Charles and Paul Goldberg, "Toward a GATT for

Investment: A Proposal for Supervision of the International Corporation," *Law and Policy in International Business*, vol. 2 (1970).

Koehane and Van Doorn, "The Multinational Firm and International Regulation," in Bergsten Fred and Lawrence B. Krause (ed.), *World Politics and International Economics*, Washington D.C. 1975, p. 191.

Krägenau, Henry, *Internationale Direktinvestitionen*, Hamburg 1975.

Kristol, Irving, "The New Cold War," *Wall Street Journal*, 17 July 1975.

Laszlo, Ervin, "The Inner Limits to Growth," *Forum for Correspondence and Contact*, V-67 (1979).

Lazarus, C. (ed.), *L'entreprise multinationale face au droit*, Paris 1977.

Levinson, Charles, *Vodka-Cola*, Paris 1977.

Lewis, Wilfred, "East-West Economic Relations," *OECD Observer*, no. 92 (1978), p. 3.

List, Friedrich, "Outlines of American Political Economy," in *Friedrich List, Schriften, Reden, Briefe*, vol. II, Berlin 1931.

Mestmäcker, Ernst-Joachim, "Recht und ökonomisches Gesetz — Über die Grenzen von Staat, Gesellschaft und Privatautonomie". Baden-Baden 1978.

Meyer, Klaus, "Die zweite Konvention von Lomé — Die Europäische Gemeinschaft und die Nord-Süd-Frage", *Europa-Archiv* Vol. 1 (1980), pp. 11-20.

Moynihan, Daniel, "The United States in Opposition," *Commentary* no. 59 (1975), pp. 31-44.

Mondale, Walter F., "Beyond Détente: Toward International Economic Security," *Foreign Affairs*, vol. 53 (1974), p. 1.

Montbrial, Thierry de, "For a New World Economic Order," *Foreign Affairs*, vol. 54 (1975), pp. 61-78.

Mosler, Hermann, *Die Erweiterung des Kreises der Völkerrechtssubjekte*, Zeitschrift für ausländisches öffentliches Recht und Völkerrecht, vol. 22 (1962), p. 1.

Myrdal, G., *Economic Theory and Underdeveloped Regions*, London 1957.

Nye, Joseph S., "Multinational Corporations in World Politics," *Foreign Affairs*, vol. 53 (1974), p. 153.

Organisation for Economic Co-operation and Development (OECD), *Code of Liberalisation of Capital Movements*, Paris 1973.

Foreign Investment in Yugoslavia, Paris 1974.

Interfutures (Final Report), Paris 1979.

Interim Report of the Industry Committee on International Enterprises, Paris 1974.

International Investment and Multinational Enterprises, Paris 1976.

International Investment and Multinational Enterprises, Review of the 1976 Declaration and Decisions, Paris 1979.

Investing in Developing Countries, 3rd ed., Paris 1975.

Mergers and Competition Policy, Paris 1974.

Penetration of Multinational Enterprises in Manufacturing Industry in Member Countries, Paris 1977.

Policy Perspectives for International Trade and Economic Relations ("Rey Report"), Paris 1972.

Peccei, Aurelio, "An interpretation of world situations and prospects," *Forum for Correspondence and Contact*, vol. 9 (1978), p. V-91.

The Human Quality, Oxford and New York 1977.

Perlmutter, Howard V., "The Tortuous Evolution of the Multinational corporation," *Columbia Journal of World Business*, vol. 4 (1969), p. 11.

Petersman, Ernst U., *International Economic Development Law: Myth or Reality?*, Law and State, vol. 15 (1977), pp. 7-37.

Portes, R., "East European Debt in Long-term Perspective," (mimeo.) 1977.

Reuber, Grant L., *Private Foreign Investment in Development*, Oxford 1973.

Ries, Charles, "The New International Economic Order: The

Sceptics' Views", in Sauvant and Hasenpflug, *The International Economic Order*, Boulder 1977.

Roberts, B.C. and B. Liebhaberg, "The European Trade Union Confederation: Influence of Regionalism, Détente and Multinationals," *British Journal of Industrial Relations*, vol. XIV (1976), pp. 261-273.

Safarian and Bell, "Issues Raised by National Control of the Multinational Corporation," *Columbia Journal of World Business* (1973), p. 116.

Salomon, J.Y., *Science et politique*, Paris 1970.

Samuelsson, H.F., "National Scientific and Technological Potential and the Activities of Multinational Corporations: The Case of Sweden," *Report to the OECD*, Paris 1975.

Sauvant, Karl P. and Hajo Hasenpflug, *The New International Economic Order (Confrontation or Co-operation between North and South)*, Boulder 1977.

Scelle, Georges, *Précis de droit des gens*, Paris 1934.

Schaller, François, *Responsabilité de l'entreprise dans l'environnement économique*, vol. 36 (1978), pp. 53-62.

Schreiber, Phillippe, *The Proper Reach of Territorial Jurisdiction: A Case Study of Divergent Attitudes*, Georgia Journal of International and Comparative Law, vol. 2 (1972), pp. 43-54.

Schwamm, Henri, *The OECD Guidelines for Multinational Enterprises*, Journal of World Trade Law, vol. 12 (1978), p. 342.

Schwarzenberger, Georg, *Foreign Investment and International Law*, London 1969.

Seidl-Hohenveldern, Ignaz, *Die "Charta" der wirtschaftlichen Rechte und Pflichten der Staaten*, Recht der internationalen Wirtschaft (1975), pp. 237-242.

Sen, S.C., *Multinational Corporations in the Developing Countries*, Calcutta 1978.

Shonfield, Andrew, *Modern Capitalism: The Changing Balance of Public and Private Power*, London 1965.

Smith, Adam, *The Wealth of Nations*, 5th ed., London 1789.

Société Française pour le Droit International, *Pays en voie de développement et transformation du droit international*, Colloque 1974.

Södersten, Bo, *International Economics*, Norwich 1971.

Steuber, U., *Internationale Banken, Auslandsaktivitäten von Banken bedeutender Industrieländer*, Hamburg 1974.

Streeten, Paul, "Ideas in Historical Perspectives," *Internationales Asienforum* 1978, pp. 27-40.

———— "The Theory of Development Policy," in John H. Dunning (ed.), *Economic Analysis and the Multinational Enterprise*, London 1974, p. 257.

The Conference Board, *Multinationals in Contention (Responses at Governmental and International Levels)*, New York 1978.

The Fund for the Republic, *A Constitution for the World*, Santa Barbara, Calif. 1965.

Tinbergen, Jan, "The Need for an Ambitious Innovation of the World Order," in *Journal of International Affairs*, vol. 31 (1977), p. 305.

Tomuschat, Christian, *Die "Charta" der wirtschaftlichen Rechte und Pflichten der Staaten*, Zeitschrift für ausländisches öffentliches Recht und Völkerrecht, vol. 36 (1976), pp. 444-491.

Trinh, Tan Hieu, *Vers une politique de la firme multinationale vis-à-vis des pays en voie de développement*, Lausanne 1974.

Tugendhat, Christopher, *The Multinationals*, London 1971.

United Nations General Assembly, *Resolution, Charter of the Economic Rights and Duties of States*, A/Res/3281 (XXIX) (1974).

———— *Resolution, Programme of Action on the Establishment of a New International Economic Order*, A/Res/3202 (S-VI) (1974).

United Nations Department of Economic and Social Affairs, *Multinational Corporations in World Development*, St/ECA/190 (1973).

United Nations ECOSOC Commission on Transnational Corporations, "Intergovernmental Working Group: Chairman's Suggestions for an Annotated Outline of a Code of Conduct," in *The CTC Reporter*, vol. 1 (1977), p. 10.

National Legislation and Regulations Relating to Transnational Corporations, U.N. Doc. E/C. 10/8 (1976).

Report on the Fourth Session, Doc. E/C. 10/43 (1978).

Research on Transnational Corporations, U.N. Doc. E/C. 10/12 (1976) and Annex U.N. Doc. E/C. 10/12, Add. 1 (1976).

Transnational Corporations and the Pharmaceutical Industry, U.N. Doc. ST/CTC/9 (1979).

Transnational Corporations: Code of Conduct, Formulations by the Chairman, Doc. E/C AC. 2/8 (1978).

Transnational Corporations in Advertising, U.N. Doc. ST/CTC/8 (1979).

Transnational Corporations in World Development: A Reexamination, UN-Doc. E/C. 10/38 (1978).

United Nations Economic Commission for Europe (ECE), *Analytical Report on Industrial Co-operation among ECE-Countries*, Doc. Sales no. E. 73 II. (1977) E. 11.

Industrial Co-operation and Transfer of Technology between ECE-Member Countries: An Analysis of Recent Developments, U.N. Doc. TRADE/AC. 3/R. 9 (1976).

Legal Forms of Industrial Co-operation Practiced by Countries having Different Economic and Social Systems with Particular Reference to Joint Ventures, U.N. Doc. TRADE/AC. 3/R. 10 (1976).

Long-term Agreement on Economic Co-operation and Trade, Doc. TRADE/R. 351 (1977).

United Nations Industrial Development Organisation (UNIDO), *Lima Declaration and Plan of Action on Industrial Development and Co-operation*, Doc. ID/B155/Add. 1 (1975).

United Nations Conference on Trade and Development (UNCTAD), *Report of the Intergovernmental Group of Experts on an International Code of Conduct on Transfer of Technology*, Doc. TD/AC. 1/9 (1977).

Report of the Third Ad Hoc Group of Experts on Restrictive Business Practices on its Fourth Session, Doc. TD/B/C. 2/AC. 6/13 (1978).

U.S. Department of Commerce, *Foreign Direct Investment in the United States, Benchmark Survey 1974*, Washington 1976, vol. 2.

Vaitsos, Constantine, "L'attitude et le rôle des entreprises transnationales dans le processus d'intégration économique dans les pays en voie de développement," *Revue Tiers Monde*, vol. XIX, p. 234 (1978).

Van Lennep, Emile, "New Approaches to International Cooperation in a Changing and Interdependent World," *The Atlantic Community Quarterly*, p. 358-368 (1977).

Vaupel, J.W. and J.P. Curhan, *The Making of Multinational Enterprises* (Harvard Business School), Boston 1969.

Vernon, Raymond, "Multinational Enterprises and National Governments: Exploration of an Uneasy Relationship," *Columbia Journal of World Business*, Summer 1976, p. 11.

Sovereignty at Bay: The Multinational Spread of U.S. Enterprises, New York 1971.

"U.S. Enterprises in the Less-Developed Countries: Evaluation of Cost and Benefit" (mimeo.) 1970.

Vogelaar, Theodore, "Multinational Enterprises: The Guidelines in Practice," *OECD Observer*, May 1977, pp. 7-8.

Walace, Helen, William Walace and Carole Webb (eds.), *Policy Making in the European Communities*, London and New York 1977.

Wälde, Thomas, *Transnationale Investitionsverträge*, Rabels Zeitschrift für ausländisches und internationales Privatrecht, vol. 42 (1978), pp. 28-86.

Wessels, Wolfgang (ed.), *Europe and the North-South Dialogue*, Paris 1978.

Wildhaber, Luzius, "Multinationale Unternehmen und Völkerrecht, in *Berichte der Deutschen Gesellschaft für Völkerrecht Heft*" 18 (International Law Problems of Multinational Corporations), Karlsruhe 1978.

Williamson, John, *The Failure of World Monetary Reform*, Sumbury-on-Thames 1977.

Wolf, Thomas A., "New Frontiers in East-West Trade," *European Business*, Autumn 1973, p. 26.

Wolmuth, Karl, "Transnational Corporations and International Economic Order," *Intereconomics*, no. 910 (1977), p. 237.

Wolter, Frank, "A sound Case for Relocation," *Intereconomics* No. 12 (1975), p. 366.

World Bank, *World Development Report 1978*, Washington D.C. 1978.

World Development Report 1979, Washington D.C. 1979.

INDEX